THURSDAY'S
GAME

↑THURSDAY'S
GAME

Notes from a Golfer with Far to Go

Tom Chiarella

1700 Madison Road   Cincinnati, Ohio 45206

THURSDAY'S GAME
Notes from a Golfer with Far to Go

Library of Congress control number: 2004105794
ISBN 1-57860-170-3

Edited by *Jack Heffron*
Cover and interior designed by *Stephen Sullivan*
Cover photo of golf bag by *Christopher Lowry Photography*

PRINTED IN THE UNITED STATES OF AMERICA

Many of these essays appeared originally in the pages of *Esquire* magazine.
Some appeared in *Washington Golf Monthly*, and a few first appeared in *Links*
and *Indianapolis Men's Monthly*.

FOR
Gus and Walt

ACKNOWLEDGEMENTS

Thanks to David Granger, a writer's editor if there ever was one, who gave me the confidence to write about playing and to stick to the playing in my writing. I know that's a fairly obtuse statement, but I'll bet he gets it. He is the engine behind this. I am grateful every time I tee up with David Field, the greatest playing partner ever and the most generous person I know. Without Bill Kammenjar, great editor and great friend, golf writing would have been no fun at all. I've further been lucky enough to have other editors who care about writing more than about product descriptions, among them Jeff Thoreson, Lou Harry and Dave Gould. I'm indebted, in different ways, to: Billy Head, Jim Wilson, John Quinn, Bill and Gigi Fenlon, Guy Berard, Jim Smith, Roger Bailey, A.J. Jacobs, Andy Ward, Will Blythe, Martin Leren, Barbara Bean, Chris White, Lili Wright, Peter Graham, Eugene Gloria, Greg Schwipps, Joe Heithaus, Tom Emery, Wayne Glausser, Mike Sinowitz, Susan Hahn, Ted Katula, Gary Barcus, Paul Hartman, Mike, Kevin and Chris Sullivan, and to many other friends at Windy Hill Country Club. Particular thanks to my brother Peter for getting me started and to Frank for keeping me laughing. These people have all helped me to think about golf and/or writing in ways that have informed this book. Many of them appear in these pages without having asked for as much. More thanks to Jack Heffron, for striking such a great partnership with me on this book and others. Finally, to everyone at DePauw University who ever made a snide remark behind my back about being a golf writer, I invite you to jump off.

CONTENTS

In Defense of Thursdays

A CALENDAR IS A BEAUTIFUL THING. THAT RELIABLE GRID! Its lockstep progression from one box to the next! One week circles in on another, sure, and in some respects that may seem a little unrelenting, even grim. But to a golfer, every day of the week has its significance. You thank God it's Friday, then sneak in thirty-six. You crowd onto the golf course on Saturday with your regular foursome. You go to church on Sunday, then grab nine holes with your son. You dread Monday. Tuesday, well, Tuesday is league night. Wednesday, you get over the hump with a bag of range balls. But I'm here to tell you that, for golfers, Thursday is what matters.

Personally, I like to practice on Thursday, dragging my bag from its niche, shouldering it up and heading for the range, which sits right at the end of the sixth hole at my little club. Things are always slow. This is just the fact of Thursday golf. The range stays uncrowded or, better, empty. I aim my shots into my favorite tree. If I listen closely I can hear the highway. My dog sits near my shag bag. A bird flies over. In the distance I can hear blasting at the local quarry. I am a distant witness to commerce and nature alike.

When I was a kid I got this same feeling when staying home from school sick. These odd days granted me a fever-driven awareness of the way things went when I wasn't there. I recall that I was amazed by how much motion and routine I was unaware of. Garbagemen came and went. Repairmen showed up. Game shows tumbled one to the next. My mother had coffee with women I had never seen or heard of. It was like I'd pulled back the curtain and looked behind the illusion of a day. I liked the world outside of school. Still, I knew I was a trespasser. I belonged somewhere else. But I discovered that no matter how caught I was in my own routine at school, the world went on without me.

So too with the golf course. The routine progresses. Mowers come and go. Greens are tended. Flagsticks are moved. The pro gives a lesson here and there in the shadow of the clubhouse. When I stand at the edge of all this, I am amazed that I would let myself forget, for even a day, the reliable industry of a golf course, its simmering quietude, its muffled rituals.

I name Thursday the last day of the golf week because on that day, you can finally forget the weekend past: The distant Friday where you strung together three birdies for the first time in four years. The rainy Saturday, when you sank a sixty-foot snake for bogey on the eighteenth with no one watching. The Sunday scramble where no one could make a six-foot putt for the money. On Thursday, you are done with this. History. Thursday is where the golf week ends.

Even so, I'm saying Thursday is when it all begins. It is the Alpha and Omega of the golf week. It is as much a beginning as it is an end. You start planning the golf ahead. You puzzle a means of slipping out, of setting things straight, of teeing up. On this day more than any other, the weekend beckons. Yes, last weekend is just a memory. But on this one page in your dayplanner, this one square in the grid of your life, the golf journey also takes its next, unlikely step forward. You think about what lies ahead—the next round, the next course, the next foursome. It might work like this: First thing Thursday, you e-mail your friends to roust a foursome for the weekend. At lunch, you call for late tee times. In the afternoon, you juggle a few weekend commitments. And if all goes well, by day's end, Thursday opens up the golf map for the next three or four days, if not beyond. For most golfers that's about as close to golf as you get—this planning, this mapping, the certainty of eighteen holes on the horizon—to golf on a Thursday.

There are some for whom playing on Thursday seems wanton, a badge of greed, the imprimatur of excess. But it's less about greed than it is about desire. But if you're really smart, if you're really hungry, if you really have the bug, you choose Thursday as the day to play, come hell or high water.

Playing on Thursday requires that the golfer be self-consciously intrepid, as it must be set up well in advance. Schedules must be juggled. You have to make the effort to break away. You have to justify to loved ones, employees, employers. But while your Tuesday league might be permanently in your book and the Sunday swing to the new course on the north side of town is something you've been looking forward to for a month, giving yourself a solitary round on Thursday is still possible. Come on. Once in awhile, it's downright necessary.

It's important to be there on Thursday. It's too easy to put the game away during the week. The calendar drives you to do so. The commute takes it out of you. Bills pile up. There are lunch meetings to be had. One day blends into the last. In some sense, every day is a Thursday when you're at work. On a golf course, outside the various routines of work and play, Thursday really stands out.

On this Thursday I am proud to have slipped away from work. The sky is a silvery blue, the haze of springtime in its farthest reaches. My partner is an old guy whose house borders the eighth hole, and he's out for a couple of holes while walking his dog. We are hitting into the seventh green from ninety yards out. It's a shot I see two, sometimes three, times a week. A half-wedge from a line of twenty-year-old white pines. I come up short of the green routinely. Today we're both short, and the old guy suggests we hit another and we're short again.

With that, he opens up his bag and dumps a half-dozen balls on the ground at his feet. I'm going to hit it until I get it right. I look behind us. There is no one even close.

So we hit, ball after ball. And soon, the way it always does when you grind out a problem on the golf course, the shot looks all that less intimidating. Finally I stick one three feet from the pin and it clings to its spot like it was born there.

When I look up, the old guy is walking away, toward his house. The green is littered with ten or twelve balls. He isn't saying a word to me. "You leaving?" I say. "Don't forget your balls."

With that he turns to me. "I'm just going inside, " he says, "to get us some orange juice."

"Orange juice?" I say.

He turns and looks at me. "Sure. Don't you want some?"

"Orange juice?"

"A big glass," he says. "Be just a minute." He looks up, and holds out his hands. "It's Thursday. I don't have anywhere to go. Do you?"

"Nope," I say, allowing that on a Thursday there's always somewhere else to be—lunches, meetings, conferences, whatever the calendar calls for—but that sometimes you have to be where you're supposed to be, starting the calendar anew, on a Thursday, on a golf course, trespassing on your own best time.

Grinding It Out

{ PART I }

1 How It Began

IN GOLF, YOU SUCCEED IN THE SMALLEST MEASURES. Any single shot takes no more than a moment and any fool can get off a great shot. Everybody's rattled a flag, or knocked in a "field shot" for a birdie, or holed out from the sand. These are great moments, but moments are cheap.

So you work to string the moments together. One great shot, then another, and another. One hole, then two, then beyond. You build. You build. You build. Then, if you're lucky, you string enough moments to build a day.

Let me start this story on a day when nothing was built, a day when many things fell apart. In the winter of 1997 I was in a fairly serious car accident. I got T-boned from the left. From there it was the usual story: glass exploded, my head snapped, the car spun. My ears rang for two days. But I walked away and for days I counted myself lucky.

I say "lucky" because I was walking, because I was apparently unshattered. I say "days" because in the days following the accident, as the skid marks were measured, as the insurance men visited my house, as the cops told and retold me their reconstructions, the pain in my neck and back did not subside. X-rays revealed that I had ruptured discs in my neck and lower back. A year later, when my hands started going numb at work, I elected to have surgery to fuse two vertebrae in my neck via bone graft.

It was a bad deal all the way around. The surgery would take care of the numbness in my hands, but no one was sure about the pain. I wanted my hands back. I'm a writer, after all. I type. I always have. But I'm also a golfer. I hit balls, too. I figured I always would.

Ten weeks after my surgery I took my first hesitant swing with a golf club. Two weeks after that, I stood on the tee with my regular group and hit my first tee shot. I hit the ball the way your mother fluffed a pillow. It wobbled 150, maybe 175, yards. I looked up at my buddies. "How'd that look?" I said.

"Like it hurt," said my friend David, and he was right. It did hurt. And it would for another six months, until I had just about given up on golf altogether, though everyone—my doctor, my physical therapist, my wife—insisted I should stay at it. When winter came, I quit.

The next spring, one full year after the surgery, I started playing again. Slowly. Now the pain rode just beneath the surface of the game, and I found that if I walked and didn't carry a bag, I could play eighteen and cobble it together for an afternoon at a time. So I pulled a cart and found ways to stay loose as I played, but I could never maintain a game or manage a full day. I was good for one hole, or three, or sometimes two good sets of three holes, but never a full eighteen. It was a spotty series of moments, nothing more. I couldn't remember what it was like to post a score, to play solidly. The center would not hold.

Then one day, three friends and I climbed in our car, the way golfers do, and drove to a distant county to play golf at a course we had heard about. There was much talk and a little music along the way, but no one went there chasing anything more special than a long look at a good course and some time with the boys.

One the first hole I chipped in for a par, followed that with two more pars, then on the par-three fourth, I jammed the ball six feet from the cup and rolled it in like it was my job. When I lifted that ball from the cup, I figured this was my moment for the day. Bang. A solid birdie, one under after four. A hawk slid across the sky. I was there.

Then I realized I hadn't thought once about my hands, or my neck. Not once in four holes. The "moment" itself had extended beyond the one shot, beyond the one hole even, into the better half of the first side. Why did it have to end? I pushed on and tried not to concentrate. Not on the pain. Not on the shots. Not on the sound of the highway in the distance. Things piled up. A nice gust pushed along a five iron. I lofted one tremendous save from behind a large greenside berm. I got a break and made a thirty-footer fall. I closed the side one under.

Since the operation, and the accident before that, I had been looking for the time when I would feel I was myself again, that time when I wouldn't worry about my injury or its aftereffects. I'd been waiting for a full day, an entire round, to show me I still had something. This was to be the day, I decided.

Then on the tenth, I took a double and followed that with another. Oddly, this didn't devastate me. I'd put the first nine together; I knew I could collect myself. I don't know that I did, but I got to the sixteenth at five over. I hadn't broken eighty since the accident. The number meant something to me. It always had. It still does. It seemed within reach. The hole was a dogleg left with a broad creek running along the left side. Son-of-a-bitch if I didn't pull my tee shot into the creek just like that. I had cranked it, but it was clearly in. The boys groaned.

I took my drop at the bend in the dogleg, and one of my friends joined me before I hit. He urged me to work for the bogey. It was good advice. A knock-down four-iron, a solid wedge, and who knew? I might still be alive. But I yanked out my three wood, and once again, he groaned. I laughed.

"Why throw away a whole day for one shot?" he said.

For the first time in more than two years, I was ready to risk it. I was confident that it wasn't just about a fleeting moment. I wasn't throwing away a whole day; I was grabbing hold of a whole day.

I took the big turn, I smoked the ball, and it rose in a hiss toward the distant green. I had done something more than I thought I could—in the great scheme, nothing but the smallest measure of a small success. It was all I'd ever wanted from the game, and all I want still. In that moment, my day was made.

2 The Range Dog

MY LITTLE CLUB HAS NO REAL DRIVING RANGE. That is, we don't have buckets of balls, slotted tokens, towering nets, nor the brave guy in the caged cart who drives in the smooth, even zamboni-strips of the ball collector, even as teenagers target him for assault with knock-down 5 irons. There are no mats. No target greens. No reliable yardage markers.

In many ways, this makes my club a less desirable choice, since I have always been a range-dog. There is nowhere I'd rather be in the failing light of a Thursday evening, then at the range, tuning a seven-iron, playing solely against my last swing. The true driving range is a beautiful spot, not aesthetically so, but spiritually, manned as it is by the hopeful and the disciplined, the ingénue and the old pro alike. At the range, it's hard to follow individual shots; we judge only by the shape and style of the player's swing. There are the constants. The smoothest players are the most focused. The fussiest players are the most ragged. The big guys swing too hard and balls are topped with a surprising regularity. The outliers are always there—the huddled groups of kids, the guys drinking beers, the informal lessons, the husband-wife pair. These are the citizens of the range. Individually and collectively, they are on their way to somewhere else—to the course for a round, to the clubhouse for a drink, or simply onward towards the better game that every golfer assumes as a birthright.

So I don't have a range to work with, not in the traditional sense. What my club does have is a large field, where members can shag their own balls. It's 260 yards to a line of trees, perhaps 280 if you hit from the very far edge of field. The field is bisected by a line of tilted and windblown distance markers. There is an apple tree to the left, and a tulip tree to the right, in the distance there sits a rusting, deserted mower. Generally, I am alone.

I always take my dog, as the field is large and generally vacant. She is a five-year-old Chocolate Lab, who learned to fetch by watching me—intently, always with purpose— poke sand wedges into the tulip tree. I like this sort of broad target, one that offers a third dimension, something beyond the flat, length-by-width, surface area of a green. I shoot high into the tree at first, looking for height, for arc, for the sheer rise of a full shot and the satisfaction of its noisy descent through the leaves. Then I reclub, a try to hit into the tree hard, to strike lumber, to make noise, to show my strength, if only to the dog. Finally I flop shots to the base of the tree, my goal to land there without having touched a leaf. This is my target, these are my drills. I own them. I developed them only because I didn't want to have to walk too far to collect my balls, only because of the idiosyncrasies of this field, only because there was a tree where there shouldn't be one. They have taught me much about the nature of a target. You can look at a given green as something with some height, something with a target area more subtle than that provided by a yardage walk-off or laser sighting.

And sure, it's ugly up there at the practice field. They don't mow it enough. The equipment is rarely, if ever, replaced. It's too windy for a range. And sometimes non-members walk on for some practice, so you never know who you'll meet. The parking sucks, and the path to the field weaves on an easement between two houses, the denizens of which cast cool glances at you as you schlep your clubs between their fences.

It is void the amenities that make the typical range effortless, somewhat sweatless, and entirely a luxury. Shagging balls—whether one is chipping toward the tattered flag that sits atop the one mound, or punching four-irons into the prevailing wind—is hard work. Your pile of balls shrinks with every passing minute. You have to watch where your balls land. You are wholly responsible for your shanks. You come to the course with a shag bag full of, say, 75 balls. They tend to be much battered, filthy, clodded with dirt, riddled with grass stains. They are shag balls, the next step down from range balls, the plankton of the game, the very bottom of the golf ball food chain, one step from sinking into the turf for eons. Still, you hit them, and you are lucky if you leave with as many as you brought. Generally the bag winnows down, but sometimes you find a few rocks, left in the wake of a previous practice session. When you shag, the size and quality of your collection wavers around the related issues of luck and natural selection. Sometimes a ball is simply lost, even in the short grass, even when you're sure that it's right there in front of you. Other times a ball is simply done, kaput, unworthy of entering the aluminum throat of your shag bag. You leave these balls behind, for others—a less discerning shagger—or for the ages—the future archeologist, hundreds of years from now, unearths a puzzling sphere.

Shagging balls demands a sort of discipline, a brand of quiet patience that runs contrary to the hurry-up-and-get-ready pace of the standard, pre-eighteen, five-dollar small bucket, hit as the minutes lapse forward toward tee time. It is a form of work and its work is an art. When you shag, you visualize a world in front of you. You are the sole citizen of an undefined space. You select a target, often distant and indistinct. You swing and the result—that exact spot where the balls lands, even its roll to a finish—is difficult to read. Your lessons come through the feedback of the club, the impact of the club on the ground, the comfort of your own finish, and the arc of the ball flight. It is the purest, most responsible sort of practice, the one most akin to the game itself and all the broader lessons that it offers. You work hard, you collect your leavings, and no one is your witness.

3   The Toughest Club in the Bag

THE DRIVING RANGE IS A HARD AND LONELY SPOT. Nobody cares that you're there. Nobody wants to watch you spank mealy, used-up Top-Flites toward the broad, indifferent nets. You do your work. You scrape it. You take your best shots, and your worst, and they add up to nothing. I work the range twice a week. That says a lot about me.

One particular day last week, Tuesday, I scarred the earth for twenty minutes with my five-iron. Now there's a golf club! The German shepherd of the golf bag—reliable, intelligent, vaguely Nazish in angle and execution. I tried for a steeper descent, a harsher cut at the ball. I wanted the ball up, sought to make it lift itself, drilling down harder and harder with each swing. But I kept going chunky with the divots, then hitting it thin, then suddenly again with the pelts of rug! What the fuck. The sky, an angry blue, carried those intense, muscular insects of summer—golf balls and yellow jackets—all around me. The sun blazed. Forty balls into the second bucket, I scabbed a five-iron one more time, then whipped the club at my bag in a gesture so dry and pointless I had to laugh.

I rested my hand on the tops of my clubs, heads rising from the bag like a sled team—loyal, strong, embarrassingly capable. Who was I to own such things? Pretender. Fool. I knew that I should pull out the wedge, my most reliable weapon: swift, heavy, compact—the candlestick in my own personal game of Clue. But my back hurt. I knew, too, that I should probably quit, leave mid-bucket, and give the game up for a while. After all, I had other troubles. Memos were stacking up in my inbox, and there were issues with the plumbing in my house.

"Fuck it," I said, and with that I pulled out the one-iron: the polar opposite of the wedge. The toughest stick in the bag. Why not? The jump from the sublime to the impossible is the golfer's lifeblood. I stood in the moment, about to perform my own yearly dance with hyperbole. I felt that I deserved it, reliably blurring those lines of pleasure and punishment like a cheap fetishist.

The one-iron—the one, the butter knife, the true flat stick—is the most hellacious club of them all. Difficult to get the ball off the fairway, almost impossible to get it in the air from any sort of rough. Most people don't carry the one-iron—pussies, all—preferring instead the gimmick, the high-numbered fairway wood, TriMetaled and fully Alpha Maraged, late-night-televisioned into their hearts. "This will save you," they are told in the infomercial. Everyone wants to be saved, especially on a golf course.

To the golfer, the one-iron is legend. There's the old joke about the one-iron, the one you've heard about Lee Trevino having been hit by lightning yet pressing on. "How will you do it?" he was asked. "How will you get out there this time?"

"Easy," Trevino said. "I'll just use a one-iron. Even God can't hit a one-iron."

The club is a simple principle: the maximum reduction of angle in the club head accompanied by a longer shaft to achieve more torque and club speed. Average golfers avoid the one, opting for fairway woods instead, which tend to channel through trouble like big, slick catfish.

Swinging a one-iron is something like holding a dildo for the first time. The geometry of the thing is so completely out of scale that you can't take it seriously. Your friends are curious. They have questions. As with the dildo, they cringe a little when you pass it to them. In that moment, you see the club for what it is: long, private, scary, bound to make even the best of us feel inadequate at times.

Still, struck square, the one-iron sizzles. Forget about it. It takes a low, simple trajectory and then tears away. You must carry the one-iron. Drill it square, just once, and you'll start to feel the potential of leverage, the pleasant surprise of your own potential. You carry it the first year to get that feeling maybe three times. It's easier to use off the tee as a driving iron than it is to use off the fairway. Since it lacks the mass of a three-wood, it can be a bitch to hit out of a heavy lie. Pros use it to get the low, 240-yard carry into a long par-five hole—the kind of thing you only dream about. The pros swing it hard, for it is a muscle club. John Daly, the hardest swinger of them all, went so far as to have a "zero-iron" custom-made for his bag.

So, at the range, I concentrated on posture, club speed, and the timing of my release, trying to visualize the carry, to encounter some coming trouble in my mind's eye. Occasionally a passing car honked to interrupt my backswing. I pressed on with the one.

At about the moment I grabbed my one-iron, my neighbor, a tiny little guy named Jack Wilson, a guy who favored a blue zip-up jumpsuit and white cloth sneakers, was having a coronary six miles away, on my leafy street, across from my house. I'm told he was planting a bush when it happened.

Minutes later, my wife was on top of him, laying down the chest compressions, having been summoned, the way nurses are in these moments—the way all of us are once in a great while—to do her best, to save the fallen man. Someone dialed 911. She worked the chest while another woman blew into Jack's mouth. She stayed at it until the ambulance arrived, working for forty minutes before the EMT called the time of death. Soon, a priest was there. At one point, she broke Jack's ribs. But she ground on. That is her way. She must continue. One way or another, she finishes a job.

Miles away, I worked to keep my spine straight, my hands together. I am not ashamed of not being there. We all have to be somewhere. I was taking my shot. So was my sweet wife.

"You feel like a fool," she told me later, describing what it's like trying to revive a dead man. We were drinking wine on our porch, looking out at the spot where Jack had died, where he'd leaned against the wall of his house and left a muddy streak as he crumbled. "But you go on."

When you learn CPR, she told me, you take a class in the basement of the high school. When you do, you practice on a dummy. You are told to shake the dummy, to shout at it. "Wake up! Are you all right?" you shout at the dummy. You feel like a fool, but you go on. This is a life skill after all; inelegance must not be an issue.

While she talked, in my sad way, I was thinking about golf, about where I was when she was nobly taking her shot, trying to press life back upon this man, our friend. I could not tell her how I had been practicing for a moment myself, carrying that stinking club all those thousands upon thousands of yards, using my training, concentrating on my mechanics, breathing deeply, pressing, hoping for the best, preparing for the worst. She was teary and sad, shaken that she had broken Jack's ribs. I poured her some merlot, and I shut up about golf. Sometimes you have to. She was my hero, and analogies have their limits.

The day will come when you need a one-iron. You'll be short off the tee, beneath a juniper, on a slightly downhill lie, on the verge of crumbling, your game folding for lack of a low, hard 230-yard runner. From that spot, you won't be able to turn your three-wood over, and you could never keep the five low enough for the overhang. So you'll reach for the one-iron. You'll speak to it, too—urgings, warnings, pleas. You've been carrying it for three years now. You've used it once. Now is the time. If you're smart, you've practiced, retrained, recertified.

It is the oldest, toughest shot. The essential risk, the superior reward. At the range that day, I had taken my hacks slowly, concentrating on keeping my back rigid, my hips square. I was alone with the butter knife, the riskiest club of all. My shots throttled away from me in low, unfamiliar arcs. Occasionally, I dropped a shoulder and chunked it something awful. Then, slowing the takeaway, holding my hips in line, I would crisply snap one on a string.

Somewhere, Jack was dying or already dead. I told you this was a Tuesday. I told you where I was—alone, like any golfer, isolated, obtuse, oblivious, entirely content in the collision of stillness and motion. I was at the range, banging my one-iron, doing my work, training to save myself.

Cut to the Tuesday men's league at my little club. The sun is setting at an August pace, hot and distant, and I'm up by two with three holes to go. I'm matched against a little guy with a hinky swing and a nice touch around the greens, a guy named Mike who owns a restaurant called Marvin's and who delivers mail in the mornings along a rural route as piecework. The last time we played I missed a four-foot putt to halve the match. That was four weeks ago, but I still want a piece of him.

We're teeing up on the seventh hole, an uphill par-five dogleg left with two serious changes of elevation and a slope running side-hill from right to left. To have any kind of chance at par, you have to move the ball from right to left. Everything sets up for the hook, the shot that Mike carries in his bag like a balisong knife for use in moments just like this. As he tees it up, I can see that he thinks the door is open, that he can take me. "I used to fade like you," he says. "More of a slice, really. But I learned to shape it. There's a world of good in that. I love going left around that corner."

I grunt. Little bastard! Gaming me when I'm up two and three. Still, looking down the chute, I can see that he's right. I need a draw here, a pronounced pull from right to left, to slam the door shut on his foot. I need to be able to shape my shot, if only for moments like this, when someone is insinuating that I slice the ball, questioning my mechanics, my self-control. So without a nod to Mike's continuing chatter, I make my adjustments, the tiny moves that golfers learn—a quarter-inch here, a visible knuckle there—to shape my shot.

I can't tell you how an air conditioner works. And though I understand water displacement, hell if I can say why a steel boat doesn't sink like a block of cement. Flight is a larger mystery still, but I'll climb aboard a Whisperliner as a basic article of faith, without a worry in my head. My home is full of perfectly reliable little mysteries—fabric softeners, smoke detectors, Krazy Glue—things I buy over and over again without ever studying them, let alone understanding how they work. You could say I don't understand much about the world around me, but I'm here to tell you: These things work.

Conversely, I do understand the golf swing. I can recognize a smooth swing from three hundred yards. I know all about the closed face, the movement from inside to out, the cocking of the wrists. I am totally down with the release. I know about gripping the club like a tiny bird, about the big turn, swing planes, and head speed. Like any golfer, I read, and then read some more: how to fix my flaws, slow my takeaway, and lead with my hips.

Still, in golf knowledge is not necessarily power. I know of fifty-three corrections I can make on my swing each time I stand over the ball. Fifty-three. I just counted. Grip. Hands. Wrists. Shoulder tilt. Hips. Knee flex. Chin. The list goes on.

Most times, it's the same story. I hit a high fade, the most pedestrian tee shot of them all. It's a whittled-down slice, really, moving gently from left to right, smothering to a spinning stop on the right side of nearly any fairway.

The fade is not a particularly ugly shot. Jack Nicklaus hit a fade all his life, and he did okay. The PGA Tour has a number of left-to-right hitters who make pretty good scratch, including the coolly spectacled David Duval. On an average course, six or seven holes are set up specifically for the fade. Like most golfers, I play the shape of my shot off the tee, lining myself up slightly left, banking on the action of my shot to take me to the center of the fairway. I live with my fade.

But the truth of the matter is that the draw—moving from right to left, with topspin adding distance to the roll—is the preferred flight path. Look at the nomenclature. The word "draw" indicates a pulling of a string, a wholly conceived and executed act. In its more exaggerated form, the draw becomes the hook—a word that suggests a weapon or, at the very least, a punch—again, a fully conceived act. The hook is long, dangerous, macho. By comparison, the fade connotes a gradual leaking of power, a sense of diminishing return, an eventual disappearance. The slice, the most extreme version of the fade, is the ugliest event in golf. The word itself—slice—is weak and passive, bringing to mind breads and pies and kitchen knives. The term "a mean slice" sounds accidental, dangerous, and hurtful, like a deep wound from a jagged piece of metal. Hard, low, and short, the slice spins like a poorly tossed boomerang, too weak to get all the way there, too shyly hit to come home. It settles halfway there and halfway back, in the repellent middle ground of the rough or the hazard.

My regular group is mostly guys who play the draw. They are a real menagerie. My cousin Marty hits the way antelopes run: smooth, fast, rhythmic. His steep, deeply tempoed swing leaves a wisp of a divot, barely marking his passage. He imports baby clothes and he's got a draw.

My friend Wayne, who took up the game just three years ago, swings limber, almost floppily, like an ostrich. He bends his arms so much you could open a jelly jar in the crook of his elbow. Still, he hits it hard, makes corrections at impact. He teaches British literature and he's got a draw.

I also play with a guy named Jaws who swipes so viciously at the ball that he could be mistaken for a rabid bobcat. Yet when he hits it solid, his ball rises and, at the very top of its trajectory, turns over to the left. Always left! The guy coaches soccer and he's got a draw.

Then there is Jere, whose mechanics are so strong, whose understanding of the game is so rich, that he can look at any shot and think: How do I shape this? For him, the game is one of possibilities, not repetitions. He makes adjustments, strengthening his grip for a draw, opening his stance for a fade. He's AC/DC. He goes both ways. He thumps us all.

Golf is a game of shapes. You stand at the first tee of a new course, and the first hole presents itself to you, tree lines bend away, fairways slope outward, spaces narrow then open in anticipation of flight paths, greens sit in geometric certainty in the distance. When you examine the card, the course is there in tiny drawings, shapes inside of shapes, shades inside of shades. You learn to regard the shape of your shot as just another certainty, as a way of fitting yourself into the place.

Standing at the seventh hole, with Mike reminding me of the

ghost of my slice, I make the moves I must in order to have any chance of turning the ball over, of hitting a draw. I strengthen my grip, rotating my right hand counterclockwise. I close my stance a bit. I remind myself to keep my hips quiet. I think of myself as a clockface, my hands falling from twelve to six, and I want to make contact just past six. I urge myself through a practice swing, thinking only of the release, the moment of impact when, if all goes well, I get to the ball with my club's face slightly closed and my hands slightly behind the ball.

Before I hit, I turn to Mike, who is gazing at the fairway ahead of us. He's banking on my rightward drift. It's his only chance—that I will throw a ball out to the right and panic over my second shot. Poor bastard.

I'm feeling good. When I hit it, I know that I've gotten through it, and when I look up, I expect to see the ball tugging leftward. As usual, it doesn't go that way. Interestingly, it doesn't curl in either direction. The ball falls gently on the center cut. Mike's shoulders sag as we approach our second shots. "There's nothing wrong with that," he says. "Straight works well, too." On the green next to us, a howl comes up as someone nails a long putt. He's right. That's when the game's simplest truth reveals itself. In the game of curves and textures, straight is surely the best shape of them all.

4   Playing Alone

I'M DROPPING BALLS ON A TEE BOX, IN THE RAIN, ON a Monday, hitting the same shot over and over again. One four-iron followed by another, then another. What can I tell you? It's the thirteenth hole on this public course I love in Terre Haute called Hulman Links, a par-three 185 yards of carry to a really nasty green, guarded on either side by these ragged, overgrown maples. You'd call the rain, at most, a light drizzle, and I can play here all day for twenty-six bucks. I'm all by my lonesome, into my second round, playing singleton, working hard at this point not to catch up to the twosome that slipped in front of me several hours ago. At the same time, I'm concentrating on staying ahead of any foursomes that may be gaining on me. I've just played thirty holes on my own. No sense screwing with the karma. I want to be alone. I drop a ball, take a look, swing. Grab another club, move to the next tee box, drop another, take a look, swing. There isn't a soul in sight. This is precisely the idea. I'm playing solo.

Playing by yourself is one of those pleasures golf offers that no other sport does. You can shoot baskets on an empty playground. You can rent a batting cage for an hour, or you can hit tennis balls shot at you from one of those hideous cannons, but none of that is made to last; none of that is anything more than a warm-up for the real thing. Only golf offers you, just you, the whole game. And let's face it: If you can't play alone—if it just isn't possible for you to grab your bag and walk nine holes by yourself once in a while—then maybe you just don't get it. Any of it.

Golf has moments some people might consider ugly, or sad. A guy standing alone in the rain on a Monday, hitting shot after shot in order to avoid the possibility of pairing up and the associated prospect of a little conversation, might qualify as pathetic in certain circles. But hey, today I'm grumpy, I'm playing well, and I just don't have it in me to be impressed by somebody else's lame attempt to shape a tee shot. I have no interest in reading the green for anyone else. Or whistling praise for someone else's short game. Or poking around in the woods for his used-up Pinnacles. I want to be alone. That's why I came out here six hours ago. Before anyone else had even seen the parking lot, I smoked my first drive into a dark mist, into the gloam, as they say—the night gloam, really, because it was still night in so many ways. The moon. The silence. The rustlings in the dark bushes. Raccoons or possums or I don't know what. But in that moment, it was just us, and I was one of them, playing.

That first shot was an act of faith. I paced it off by feel and without fear of penalty. But I found that ball, and the next one, too. And pretty soon the sun rose a bit, and then it started to rain, and it was as if I had awakened there in the middle of the third hole, as if it were one of those dreams that you can extend by hitting the snooze button. Only, for me, those dreams involve the prospect of sex, and here on the course I was alone. That was how it was going to be all day.

Minutes pass. Footsteps fall. You see great things. A hawk. A catfish, big as a sewer pipe, drowsing beneath the skin of the water. An army of crickets at your feet. Even your own drive, working itself toward straightness, rising righteous and silent like those in the highlight films. This is golf. Fully and completely. It doesn't matter that no one's there to see it.

All that said, it's important to note that a singleton is a real pain in the ass to other people on the course. From the perspective of a foursome, there is nothing worse than seeing some schmoe humping a bag of overbeaten clubs all by himself. I'm not arguing against the right to play your own little solo round. Feel free. Just keep me out of it.

The first time you see a singleton is like the first time you get a good look at a deer. You stop for a moment; you stare. The creature looks pretty much as you expected: fearful, muscular, overly careful perhaps—you might even call it beautiful or noble. But the tenth time you see one, you think, holy shit, there are a lot of those things around here, and you pretty much wish someone would shoot it before you end up crashing into it.

On a normal day, tucked into the number-two slot of my normal foursome, the vision of a solo golfer gaining on us is met with groans and a familiar chorus involving dubious golf legalese.

"A singleton doesn't play through," Wayne always says.

I agree. "A singleton has no rights."

"Not over a foursome," Wayne adds. "That's a rule."

It's at about this point that Jere, who goes it alone once or twice a week, makes himself heard. "When I was a boy, I always enjoyed playing alone, and I always played fast."

Mike, who is as passionate about golf etiquette as I am about milk, sighs. "Come on. Let's wave him through. Otherwise, he's back there just, I don't know, just watching us."

It's about then that we all consider the guy, bobbing back and forth on the distant hill.

"Looks like he can swing," I say.

"I don't like singletons," Wayne says. "I mean, come on. Call somebody up. Get a game. Don't come out here like it's meditation or something. You know what I mean?"

I stick my hand in the air, wave the guy through. We shoulder our bags and step to the side. The guy, standing 180 yards out, sticks a dart on the green eight feet from the cup. He approaches quickly, jogs to the green, lips out the putt. Then he turns to us and gently says what they all say: "Thanks, guys." He's off the next tee before any of us sinks a putt. "That guy can play," Wayne says. "I just hope he's the last of them."

He isn't, of course, and neither am I. But here, on this lousy Monday, I have become what I beheld. I am the singleton. I've hit twelve balls, three from each tee box, in an attempt to gain some distance control. Four of the balls sit indifferently on the massive green. Four are gone forever. The rest are in some layer of trouble—sand or bush or gravel. Finally I hit one from the ladies' tee or from a retired drop area; I can't be sure. The ball jumps straight up, gains a track, eases downward, and smacks the bottom of the flag like a cue ball on the break.

I can't see the ball. I can't see it! And I'm jumping up and down to see if it fired off into the woods. But it's a hole in one. I feel sure of it. Sort of. More like a hole in thirteen, really. But it was one shot. It could be called something like a hole in one, anyway, if there were somebody there to name it for me. I turn in a circle, looking for a witness—someone to tell the story for me. I shout out. I need a witness. But this is Monday, in the rain, deep on a rural golf course, and I am all alone.

⑤ Winter Rules

THE FIRST TIME YOU PLAY GOLF, YOU'RE PRETTY much naked. You wear strange clothes. You slip on a single glove. Then you're forced to tee off in front of strangers. Dark, knowing silhouettes bob in the window of the pro shop. You twist yourself like a fool, sadly mimicking the waxy, smooth game you've seen on television. You are a rakish, public clown.

Still, you can stand it. It's summer. The sun shines and some-one lights a cigar. You start to accept that no one much cares what you do, no matter how public it all seems.

But play golf in the winter, on a sunny February day in, say, Illinois, and you're on your own in a different way. The pro shop is closed. The tee markers are in the shed. Snow crusts the cart path. It's beyond quiet. Men are drinking coffee and slipping on two gloves. The trees are bare, the greens ringed in brown. Now no one watches you, even the guys you play with. You tee off into a kind of friendly abyss. You walk quickly, though there's no one behind you. You are playing winter golf, the most private game of them all.

Once in a while, I drag my brother-in-law Jim out for some winter golf. He's a huge lug, a lawyer, born and bred in Dade City, Florida, who knocks the ball as long as a body can, dropping down on top of it as if swinging a huge ax, arcing the ball on a high, hard draw. He's an agreeable guy, the kind of person who'll ask questions about your job and actually listen for a while, who'll buy you gin drinks from the beer cart, a guy who loves Southeastern Conference football. He plays a fast round of golf, and he goes easy on the advice. All around, a good playing partner. But he's from Florida, and you have to kick him to get him to bring his clubs above the panhandle. He likes his golf like shitty British beer: just plain warm. Set a nipple-hardening wind to blowing and cloud the sky with big, milky January clouds, and he whines like a worn fan belt.

When we played my father-in-law's course in Tennessee last December, it was no more than forty degrees outside when we started. Then it grew colder. Jim had consented to play at the last minute, and I didn't turn back when, at the trunk of the car, a snowflake wobbled downward between us. It had been six weeks since I'd played, and I was hungry for it. I offered him some Chap Stick and figured he could suck it up.

By the second hole, Jim was muttering to himself. "I just don't get this," he said as his short putt rumbled across the spike-pocked green and past the hole. "What's the attraction?"

"You have to keep moving," my father-in-law said, thumping his arms against his chest. He's a tough little guy named Billy with a harsh, low swing and a follow-through so hard that his foot comes off the ground, sometimes sending him lurching backward like a drunk. Still, he's straight as an arrow to the green, and he could putt a taut line across a gravel parking lot in a rainstorm. He sold aluminum products for almost thirty years. The cold is nothing to him. Jim didn't want any part of it. On the tenth hole, Billy turned to me and said, "Ol' Jim's not too happy." I looked back. Jim paced along the right side of the fairway, his head wrapped in two white golf towels, the uppermost of which was skid-marked with a slash of turf.

"Jim," Billy said, "you want a hat?"

He patted his head. "All set," he said.

Neither of us had the heart to tell him it looked as if he were wearing a helmet of toilet paper. When he hooked his second shot into the scrubby pines a moment later, he had the bag on his shoulder before the ball came to rest. "Let's put an end to this," he said. This was his way of asking if we wanted to quit. Personally, I was laying one 108 yards from a fat green with a generous pin placement. Screw him. "Wear wool," I wanted to tell him, "and shut your pie hole." I wasn't going anywhere. About then, it started to snow. I could hear Jim muttering "Please" from the other side of the fairway.

I grabbed my wedge. The wind picked up. My father-in-law shouted to Jim. "Jim!" he said. "You want some gloves, Jim?"

Jim took a long blink and pulled the towels tighter around his head. "I don't think gloves are the answer."

Billy shouted back to him, "You should have gloves—90 percent of the body's heat exits through the hands."

"I think you mean head," I said.

"Hands," he said. "Most people don't know that."

I was sure he was right. My hands, ungloved, had hit the point where they seemed like only reminders of hands, mere Post-its on the ends of my arms, reading, "These are your hands." And that's how it goes in winter—the course is painful and arctic, a grim testament to the permanence of the game laid atop the somnambulant landscape of a dormant course. Winter golf wears you out, no matter how many towels you wrap around your melon.

So we were at odds, the three of us. Jim, the best golfer, was there to stumble and chatter. Truth was, we'd known he would be miserable. We'd banked on it. But here he was, lighting us up, taking the money. Jim had no out. My father-in-law had schlepped us both out to his club, so he wouldn't let the cold touch him; he wanted to rip Jim a new hole first. And me, I had basically declared myself to be mountain stock, far tougher than the cold. I was stuck, too.

The sun creaked upward, and a bird throbbed along the updrafts. I stood 108 yards away. I stuck my hands down my pants. Condensation, you know. My ball was on a thin patch of fairway. I wanted to roll it to a better spot but didn't dare ask.

I've never much cared for winter rules. Kick the ball, sure. Poke it out from under a bush. Drop a new one out of your pocket, for all I care. But don't hide behind some notion of those dopey winter rules.

Play it as it lays, then get moving.

I looked at Jim then. The wind was rolling now. He was pressed up against a pine tree, his forehead tilted downward. It appeared that he had given up, that he was giving in to the cold, to the lunacy. For a moment, I thought we should quit. Then I looked down the fairway and caught a glimpse of Billy's ball landing on the green and jumping up to within twenty feet of the pin. I could feel it, then. I wasn't going anywhere, except to the flagstick on the two-hop express. I was staying.

You play winter golf when that ache gets too bad, when you have to get a sense of what you've lost in the dark, cold months of winter, when you want even the dimmest doppelganger of summer. You layer on the clothes. You carry the bag the way a mountain man carries a buffalo hide, like something purposeful and a bit smelly. You creep up on the familiar spots of summer, and they offer an entirely new challenge. The leaf-bare branches of the tight dogleg are penetrable. You begin to see the things you've wanted to do, the frames of shots that can't show themselves to you in the summer. There is something there on the golf course in winter. Sometimes you can find me there, getting ready, soothing my ache in private.

So I made my address, hummed my swing thought, and drew my club back. I could sense the frost on my beard. The grass below looked wounded and forgotten. Turning through the shot, I could see my brother-in-law look up. My frozen hands gave me the dimmest correspondence of contact. I believe the ball rose in a stiff arc. I could not tell you, as I was moving forward before it landed. Jim barked encouragement. Billy piped in about then. I didn't listen. I was dead-alone, with my golf bag and the season around me.

6 My Day

ABOUT A THOUSAND YEARS AGO THIS VERY morning, to be precise, I made my nine-year-old son three blueberry waffles in our toaster. He ate them in front of the television while I walked the dog. When I returned, he was watching a cartoon we both like called *Beast Wars*.

"How long is sixty milliseconds?" he asked me in his loose, disinterested way, staring at the screen as a hawk turned into a robot and then back again into a hawk. I knew this drill. He'd heard something. Now he was breaking it up, figuring it out. Asking questions, but not *the* question.

"Not long," I said. "A lot less than a second."

"Like an eye blink," he said.

"Less, I think."

"Like a snap," he said.

I sipped my coffee. Now another robot was riding the hawk,

beating it on the head, taunting the hawk as it careened downward.

"I don't know," I said. "I think a snap might be longer."

"You can't measure a snap," he said. He demonstrated.

"I think you can," I said. "I think you can measure just about anything."

"No matter how short?"

I nodded. I really believed it. My boy took that in. He whistled his little whistle and picked up his book bag, and we trundled off.

Every morning, I drive him to school. Depending on how late we are, we often wait in a line of cars, each nudging forward along the arcing drive, dropping one kid at a time in the single reliable designated spot. My boy refuses to get out before we hit that spot, though I have urged him to do so on occasions when we are very late. "Dad, it's a rule," he reminds me. "Schools have rules, you know."

Every morning, he leans over the seat and gives me a kiss, in plain sight of every other kid in the schoolyard, as if that were just another rule, though every morning I think that'll be the last one, the last kiss before he's too embarrassed to kiss his old man in public. Then he climbs out of the car and thumps toward the doors. I watch until he passes the principal, who waits at the doors every day, greeting each child by name, drinking his coffee from one of those massive mugs you see nowadays. I leave only when I'm sure this man has said hello, when he's used my son's name—Gus—to welcome him in. I can see other parents lingering, too, not leaving until the doors shut behind their children, dark and shiny and certain. Sometimes I can see the steam rising from the principal's coffee as I pull away.

This morning, four cars away from the drop point, Gus said, "What about one millisecond?"

"What about it?" I said.

"Could you measure that?'

"Sure."

"I bet you'd need a computer," he said.

Just before climbing out, he showed his cards, asking his real question, the thing he's worried about. "On *Beast Wars*, they were saying they could blow up the whole planet in sixty milliseconds." He kissed me, looked in the rearview mirror, and pressed down a cowlick. "Could you do that? Could you blow up a planet in sixty milliseconds?"

"I don't think so." I shook my head, pursed my lips as if it were a reasonable proposition, and said, "No, I don't think you could blow up a planet." I really believed that, too. "Don't worry," I told him, and then he was gone.

Billions of milliseconds later, that very afternoon, I was shagging balls with my seven-iron. I was pretty sure about the world. I kept scalping out the same shot, scraping the earth, sending the balls upward in throbbing arcs toward a distant orange post. This is about as far away from everything as I can get in this life, alone on a tiny practice range, at the top of a hill, beyond the last row of houses, at the north edge of my little town. In the distance, a dog barked.

It was 2:20. I'd skipped out on work and gone to bang balls before school got out for Gus. I was worried. My brother was coming in for the member-guest that weekend. My takeaway sucked. The sun was like a piece of jewelry in the sky. I had a song in my head. "I'm a lumberjack and I'm okay." I sang it to myself as I went to the pro shop for a drink. "I sleep all night and I work all day." The television was on, as it always is, and the pro's wife stood at the counter, looking past me to the screen, holding a pack of toasty peanut butter and crackers. She didn't put it down. I glanced at the screen. Information came the way it does for me at such moments, in rips and tears: a beige wall, a man crouching behind a car, smoke. A reporter spoke. "FOURTEEN DEAD," the caption read. Kosovo, I thought. Jesus. Behind me, hot dogs circled a hot bulb. Then I noticed that the screen had an unusual clearness, and the building was too new, and there was a huge parking lot of the sort you'd never see in Kosovo, especially not nestled next to a blossom of three baseball fields. The building was a school, I could see, and then I could really see, everything thrust forward all at once, in a light I can only think of now as bronze and absolute. It was a school. And for one moment, for however many countless slices of a second it took, I had this thought: I know those bricks. Those are Gus's bricks. There were letters at the bottom of the screen, smaller pieces of the story, telling me things, large things. "SCHOOL SHOOTING," the letters said.

"Now?" I said, too loud, to no one in particular. "Now?" And no one answered.

And miraculously, the first word I heard from the reporter was "Now."

It was answer enough.

When I leave the pro shop, I am headed to my son, toward his school, where I left him on that planetwide, daily article of faith. School is school, more holy for the young child than any church or synagogue. We leave our children there in the face of all we know about things, in the face of all the things they will learn there. We do it. We must. I want more of what he started that morning. I want to watch him gear things down into smaller and smaller units and let him help me figure as I notch things in the other direction. I won't tell him any of what went on in Littleton, that moment when the planet exploded in milliseconds, the first of many such explosions he will live through, I'm sure. Or I will tell it all to him. I can't be sure.

The sun shines. Like any day, the world radiates goodness despite itself.

Traffic is thin but slow. I am pulled along whatever arteries are offered me, toward my child, my boy, his school. In the days and weeks to come, I am sure, we will hear the stories of the long, torturous drives of the parents to the high school in Colorado named for the flower—Columbine. I pound the steering wheel. None of it is swift enough. None. Not one second of it. Not even in its tiniest measure.

7 And the Rains Came

MY FRIEND G. IS A NEW YORK GUY. HE LIKES $1.50 egg sandwiches and coffee bought from vendors in aluminum carts. He enjoys his hour-and-fifteen-minute commute up the Hudson river. He wears $1,400 suits to work. He eats steak. He spends most of January in Milan and Paris, at fashion shows, selling pages in the magazine he edits. G. has everything. Better said, he's well fixed. He's got what he needs. New York is like that. It provides for a guy like G.

Me? I live in rural Indiana. I buy my coffee in paper cups at the Marathon station. My bagels are imported from an exotic city called Mooresville. I walk six minutes to my office. I wear sixty-five-dollar button-down shirts from Nordstrom to work. I spend my January shoveling snow, hoping my pipes don't freeze, and playing cribbage with my car mechanic. That said, I've got what I need. Indiana provides for a guy like me.

In most ways, G. has more than I do, but we like the same things. On weekends, G. plays golf at his private club. In the failing light of a Thursday he plays golf, grabbing five, six, seven holes before the day ends. In his basement, in his laundry room, he plays golf, chipping balls off a carpet remnant into a long-forgotten pillow resting against the base of his wall. G. can't get enough golf . Neither can I. And that's where we differ.

When I say I can't get enough golf, I'm generally saying I can't play enough to get bored, tired, or unenthusiastic about the game, as in "I can't get enough shrimp scampi!" When I say "G. can't get enough golf," I mean it literally. He can't get enough. Period. Emphasis on can't. He lives in New York. There isn't enough golf to go around. What golf you can find is either too distant or too shabby, too wildly private or too crowded to be much of a factor. In the New York metropolitan area, you get what golf you can, but you don't expect much.

New York is a sort of golf purgatory, where a round on a public course is a six-hour affair, replete with the hassle of parking, the drain of the commute, and the misery of playing cheek-by-jowl with every schmoe who ever stumbled across a set of old Tommy Armour irons at a garage sale.

I've been telling G. for years to come to Indianapolis, that we'd get as much golf as we could handle in three days and leave plenty for next time. I told him Indianapolis—Indiana, for that matter—is a golf promised land, undiscovered and underrecognized. Forget New York, I told him. He'd get more golf than he could handle here in Indiana. Every time I said this, G. snorted. He was skeptical. Then, one day last spring, he told me he was coming to town.

I should pause here and say this clearly: I can get enough golf. Oh hell, I've probably had enough golf. Indiana provides that and more. Like anything really good in Indiana, you have to drive a bit, you have to know where you're going, and you have to accept that there are no real secrets. But truth be told, golf can be had here. In a given week last summer, I played twenty-seven holes at Hulman Links in Terre Haute, one of the best public courses anywhere; nine holes at my own little club in Greencastle, hewn from the side of the hill by barbers, farmers, and IBM executives; a quick morning eighteen on the grounds of Fort Benjamin Harrison; another eighteen at the Trophy Club (which has always sounded like the name of a strip club to me); and a difficult eighteen at Wolf Run, the toughest private course, well, anywhere. I couldn't get enough golf! Meanwhile G. looped his home course twice and called around for a Saturday tee time elsewhere. He couldn't get enough golf!

When G. arrived it was the third week in April. I'd pulled every string I had access to and had set us up at every primo course I could get near. Eighteen at Crooked Stick, followed by an afternoon eighteen at Broadmoor, then eighteen at the Legends in Franklin, and an evening eighteen at the Speedway course, closed out by eighteen at Coyote Crossing in West LaFayette and a final visit to Hulman Links. Six good courses in three days. It was the best I could manage. Before he got here, G. admitted that he hadn't played six different courses in Westchester County in ten years.

On the night before our first round, I congratulated myself. I was going to show the New York guy the what's what, the lowdown, the dirty truth: We have it better out here. I made reservations as St. Elmo's. I stocked my wine cellar with good wine. Who needs Manhattan? I asked myself. Right about then, the rain started.

It rained the way it does when the world wants to make you feel small. Within hours there was talk of flashfloods, tornadoes, and eastward-bearing storms hanging over Missouri. It rained the way it does when God wants to send you a message about being smug, about congratulating yourself and being too comfortable with your own personal excess. I was chastened. I didn't tell him, but when I picked G. up, I was a little bit sorry the weather hadn't closed the airport. I knew that we were doomed.

In the morning, before first light, the calls started coming in. Crooked Stick was closed. Too much water. Broadmoor, too. I told G. we could head out and play at one of the public courses, hoping he might say no, that he might want to hunker down and wait it out. After all, I did have a lot of wine. But G. is nothing if not a gamer. Besides, as I've established now, he can't get enough golf. So we crept onto the Coffin in the downpour, splish-splashing our way around the remarkably challenging little city course. Afterward, soaked to the bone and craving soup, I threw out my shoes and my pants, bought a new outfit at the proshop, and looked to the sky. Nothing was letting up. It was a little after noon. I figured we were done.

"Where to?" G. said. He wanted more. He was hungry for it. I called around. Eagle Creek, on the city's northwest side, would let us out. The pro warned me: "We're under water, so I can't let any carts out there. You're going to have to walk."

So we played. It's what you do.

I've said it before: There's a greed in golf that ought not be denied. At its worst this is a common greed, a covetousness that makes us hunger for equipage, more and better. It's the greed that makes people play courses and prove to the world that they did by collecting logoed golf balls and displaying them on oak racks.

At its best, the greed of golf is a greed for experience, a thirst for the unique challenges that each and every course offers. Every shot in golf is a fresh look at the entire game. The elements are there: an object, a man, the world around him. The action, the swinging of the club—whether in a downpour, or in a light snow, or in the full heat of a Las Vegas summer day—is the common intersection of the game. It's what makes us players. G. understands this. He would play underwater, so long as he could nut his tee shots and be assured that the greens were true. That's why they don't worry about rain in Ireland. They're players. They understand the greed, and they know the need.

G. is a player too. And so we played for three straight days in the worst rain I have ever seen in Indiana. Everywhere we went, the rain followed us. Every course was closed or reduced to limited play, and I would have to talk the pro into letting us out under curious conditions. No carts, or cart paths only. Don't walk on the greens. Play out of the rough only. Don't stand on the bridges.

At the end of those days, we had played none of the original courses I had lined up for us. Instead we'd made an amazing criss-cross of the county, of the region, really, in search of courses that would have us—the valiant little public courses that make Indiana golf so great. The Elks in Plainfield, Rolling Meadows in Gosport, the Brickyard in Speedway. I was thankful, but the rain was cruel. My skin peeled. My bones ached. Our clothes, our shoes, were ruined again and again. And yet we circled back for more every day.

When it was over, the rain stopped, of course. It always does. That's the cinematic irony of a game defined by vision, by vistas, by the adaptation of nature that a golf course represents.

When G. and I sat down at the end of it all, we were finally at St. Elmo's. G. ordered the shrimp salad. And when it came, I asked him if he'd had a good time despite the weather.

He picked up a shrimp, dunked it in the horseradish, and bit down. "Me?" he said. "Absolutely. It's good here. Lots of choices. Besides, there's no such thing as bad golf."

So I had succeeded in some small way at showing him how good it was out here.

"But," he said, crooking one finger toward the massive shrimp, the fiery cocktail sauce, pinching his nose to fight back the tears, "this is unbelievable. That's the best I've ever had." He plucked another shrimp from the edge of the glass. "I'm telling you, you can't get this in New York. I can't get enough of this."

I smiled. That's what I'd been telling him all along.

8) Multiple Choices

I'M OUT WITH MY BOY JERE, WHO HAS TRIMMED down, hooked up with some clean new Mizuno blades, and started to shoot scores. "It's really happening," he told me in the car. I believe him. It's a Thursday, and I'm out for a look. We've chosen a new course, on the south side of a large Midwestern city, arriving via the arterial throb of interstates. The sun is a clatter of light in the sky.

We're playing with a kid Jere likes named Ryan, a self-serious chemist from the local pharmaceutical giant. The kid is in his early twenties. He makes three times what I do. His handicap is five times lower than mine. Worse still, he's brought his boss along. This guy is a chop. He's a little round, very bald, toting a bag full of A-plus clubs. Watching him swing at the range beforehand, I decide it's good he's here, since he takes me off the hind tit. I'm third best in our little crew, not the captain or even the mate. Just the trusted seaman, the experienced pirate, ready to gut the new guy if he eats more than his share of the rations.

In golf, your whole day is a series of choices. Global, geographic choices—where you play, with whom, in what weather—and smaller, more obscure ones—angle of your shoulders, length of your tee, the ball you play—all of which produce an alchemy akin to soup. Sometimes you can't get enough, bowl after bowl, and other times you wish you'd ordered the club sandwich instead. Today's a sandwich.

Four holes in, it's the usual story. My scores look like a string of zits along the shoulder blade of an adolescent. Double, double, par, bogey. I'm playing the way I did twenty years ago. I'm playing the way I did last week. I'm playing the way I will three days before I die. Forgetting everything I've learned, worked on, practiced, and otherwise pushed into my blood. I can't choose to play differently. The kid is level par, Jere is one over. Meanwhile, the boss, the cabin boy on our voyage, is only one stroke back of me. I'm dying here. I bomb a five-iron over one green, I leave a six short on the next. By the seventh hole, I can't make a choice at all. Decisions are beyond me. My hands touch every club in the bag, and not one feels right. Jere walks with Ryan, leaving me to find my jittery, half-assed drives along the right side (always the right!) in the second cut, 60, 70, 130 yards behind them. And I'm walking with the boss. He is huffing and puffing, kicking around the same grass as me. We are, I'm feeling, not all that different.

On one par-five, he's three hundred yards from the green and he can't decide between a three-wood and a two-wood. He doesn't have a prayer, and he wants all my spare Hail Marys. I shrug.

When you're aiming, you picture the shot rising at a certain arc, steep and elegant or low and supple, always with a shape as subtle and purposeful as a woman's back. When all is right, the club matters. Moving from an eight to a nine has a profound effect. The right choice stiffs the flag. You view your bag as a series of controlled choices. When things are going badly, though, every club looks like a face in the crowd—distant, indistinguishable, more than a little vacant—and you're playing Where's Waldo with your $750 fitted Pings.

I've got the same shot as the boss. But I'm no help. I have quandaries of my own. I'm broke. I'm getting a divorce. I want a new job. I get out of bed only when my dog pees on the floor. I can't hit a fairway wood to save my life. Besides, it's golf. Decisions are private. From one cabin boy to the other, I'm saying, "Don't ask me. I can't make up my mind about anything." Besides, he hasn't given me any advice. Why would I help him? He ends up hitting a four-wood, and I choose a five-iron, and neither one of us is right. I'm eleven over at the turn; he's thirteen over, jabbering on about how he broke fifty. I sulk, create some distance, have a conversation with myself in which I outline the appropriate excuses. Things go better on the back, and I finish just four over for the nine.

So we shake hands, and they want to have beers, Jere and the kid, to rehash their seventy-twos. The boss, who shot a 103, is game. Me, I want to sit in the car with my arms folded. But I tag along because Jere will surely buy. The tables in clubhouses are where you finally feel your body after a round, where you pass your money, where you ultimately look your opponents in the eye. The boss takes off his hat. The top of his head is as ruddy as his face.

The small talk picks up. Eventually I mention my divorce. The boss perks up.

"How long have you been split?" he asks me, pressing the glass of AmberBock to his forehead like a poultice. Six months, I tell him. He nods. "Want some advice?" I don't think I even nod, because I know he'll give it anyway. Everyone does. In divorce, your choices are shockingly public.

"Stop being mad," he says.

I tell him I'm not particularly mad.

"Sure you are," he said. "All divorced people are mad at first. It's just the way it is." I shrug.

"It won't work if you wait for it to wear off," he said. "You have to make a choice. A decision. Like, 'Today I'll stop being mad.'"

I lean back. "Just like that, eh?"

"Get on with it. Make the choice and get on with it. The minute you stop being mad, things will happen."

So there I am—reticent, bone-tired, nursing a club soda and lime. Jere and Ryan aren't saying anything. The moon will rise soon enough. For the first time today, I can hear this guy. Now I'm vaguely glad I met him. He may have given me something just now, and playing with him is suddenly a happy accident, one of those reliably human collisions that golf produces. I can see why he's the boss. I'm looking out the window. I may even turn back to him and meet his eyes. It's my choice, my decision. Any minute now, I'll make it.

9   My Favorite Club

THE FOUR-IRON SHOULD SCARE YOU. YOU SHOULD pull it from your bag with trepidation. It's long and it's nasty, this first step out of the middle irons. You need a four only when you're perched against failure, standing at a distance long enough to look just beyond reach or just within. That uncertainty makes the club what it is. A test. A trial. A benchmark. The four-iron makes you prove who you are on the golf course.

The first time I ever really cranked a four I was by myself at a little club in the Midwest. The rain was just starting to fall, and I was headed in to the clubhouse, a singleton playing on a guest pass. Having shot left off the tee, I faced a long carry to an elevated green, about 190 yards out. I needed to jump a row of hemlocks about thirty yards away and the wind was blowing straight across. Neither too high then, nor too low, the shot represented to me a really good knock. I have to admit I was tired and a little bored, so when I took out the four-iron, I did it with "hell with it" attitude. I wanted to get there and get out. The club had never been much of a weapon for me—too long, too risky, and I too prone to mistake. Still this time, I swung loosely and paused when the ball rose quick and mean as a missile. I said something to myself, something like "Yes." The ball just seemed to get swifter and harder as it bore down on the flag. The wind was no issue and the hemlocks didn't matter. I had just hit a good four-iron. The ball tracked, hit once, and rolled to within three feet. I yelped, though there was no one there to hear me.

I stood on that rise, hitting the club for about ten minutes, wanting more. But the four just wouldn't give it up. I'd had a taste and that was all. Years later, I still like to bring the four out of the bag, still like to bear down in hope that I will catch it flush. I'm guessing now, as I was then, that I don't know that outside edge of my four-iron. Not many of us do. For me, it represents everything that makes golf what it is. It is the steely weapon, unafraid of the wind, unafraid of distance, difficult and more than a little bit scary; it's the way the game ought to be.

10 Playing with Trouble

IT IS THURSDAY, AND I AM CLINGING TO THE EDGE OF a steep, wet hill above a dank lake full of oversized frogs. I am hooked tenuously to the ground by the cleated soles of my shoes. My hips are at an angle I've never experienced before, tilted forward and out, as if I were about to drop a child from between my legs. My legs are spread, my shoulders dropped. I am about to hit a six-iron off a steep downhill, sidehill lie. *Knees*, I'm thinking, *bend your knees*. But the truth is, this is just something I heard once, something that makes me feel more secure in what I'm about to try.

My knees have nothing to do with it. At this moment my toes might be the sole element of balance in my life, the only force keeping me from tumbling backward onto my ass or lurching forward into the pond.

To play golf, you are constantly pressed against new impossibilities. Beneath trees, from the edges of cliffs, on the faces of the slipperiest slopes, you bend and twist, torqued against your limits, against the skin of the world on which you stand. Still, you set your feet and try.

Moments ago, I had a choice: a safe chip to the middle of the fairway or a risky six-iron lofted left to right toward, I hoped, the marrow of the green. I shrugged and chose the six, opting for this goofy dance with my own bones. The body protests shots like this. My neck hurts, my shoulder is tight, my hands are starting to blister, my knee aches, and the angle of my ankle is just plain wrong. My damp feet are starting to peel inside my shoes.

My brother Peter has a lot he'd like to say about my predicament, but he's standing behind me, arms crossed, biting his lip, bouncing slowly on his toes. He's done this sort of ballet before. Just two holes earlier he climbed into a stand of pine trees, hooked one foot behind the branch of a tree, hunched his shoulders under a thorny overhang, and chopped a ninety-yard one-iron shot under a row of hemlocks. "You're sure you want to do this?" he says now.

Normally, I'd consider this comment gamesmanship, but he is legitimately concerned that I will look like a fool or, worse, hurt myself. I appreciate that, especially since he has a smear of pine sap across his cheek. I'll take my shot.

People complain about the overly manicured nature of golf courses, about the preciousness of the game itself. Ironically, though, all the other sports are the ones that are completely denatured. You could play tennis on a runway at LaGuardia. And don't tell me baseball. In the majors, they rake the infield until it looks like a pool table. Derek Jeter might get a bad hop once every three weeks, but even then there are twelve guys waiting with hoses to make sure it doesn't happen again. Football? Come on. Those guys play on AstroTurf.

In golf, every shot is vaguely distorted by the angle of the earth, by the texture of the particular piece of turf on which the ball comes to rest. You might hit the perfect tee ball on a par-three and, because of the slope, find that it has come to rest just off the green—forty feet from your ultimate goal—and now you must place one foot at an angle against a downhill slope, toes three inches above heels, one knee bent, the other locked straight. You accept it. You are a golfer. You twist yourself against the shape of the world.

In this way the game is distinctly and absolutely physical. No, you aren't boxing anyone out, and you aren't driving the lane. There are no diving catches. You never run, and you only rarely duck. The game is about a different kind of response, the way your body deals with the tasks at hand, which are different for each shot, each lie, and each course—on every day you play.

On this shot, I expect nothing from my hands and everything from my back, from my ass, from my legs. I am leaning backward while swinging forward. I feel as if I am about to chop myself into two halves. And worse: I'll end up in the water. Peter says so. "Dude, I wouldn't want to fall into that," he says of the murk below me. "Chip out." We're on two-dollar Nassaus, and as usual he's chewing me up. Chip out, my ass.

Sometimes you work on faith rather than physics. You trust that your body will get you through. The clubhouse sages, the bookshelf gurus, tell you to back off these moments. Gear down, choke up, chip out. Play it safe. It is a familiar drone. But you must try, you must test yourself, you must let yourself play these moments against the planet itself, if nothing else.

I have seen men hit from both knees (four times), standing with one leg knee-deep in a bog, hanging at their belt line over the branch of a tree, and otherwise leaning against trees, rocks, and fence posts. Countless times, I have seen people fall on their asses after hitting from a wet lie or hillside. I once played with a guy at an Elks Club outing who broke his wrist hitting from atop a tree root. I have seen shots from every angle set upon the tops of cliffs, from the center of a beach, from deep inside gravel pits and creek beds. My college roommate once reached both arms around a thirty-year-old ginkgo tree in a weirdly sexual fashion and knocked a ball onto the green. Such is the yoga of the game.

If you need a flat lie, go play Putt-Putt.

So, there at the edge of the lake, I step in and address the ball, which seems yards beneath me, held in that spot only by the dew. I tick off a reminder or two, then quit. The hell with it. I'll take my aim. This won't look good, but I am willing to shed the elegance of the game for a moment, to puzzle out my particular circumstance, to see the challenge I face right now, at this juncture, in this wind, on this rock. My brother moans in the background. But I have to believe that I can do it, that I have worked on my game if only to understand shots like this. Besides, I am strong and I am willing to take the fall, if only for this one great, unlikely shot, the smallest measure of glory the game can offer.

11 The Cheater Within

YOU HAVE TO LIKE A HANDICAP CARD. The sheer string of numbers, the record of round upon round pressed into chronological order, ranked and inserted knowingly into a vaguely obscure formula, producing one solid number, one point on the X-axis of our golf lives that says: Here, this is where you stand. You are a twelve. Or a four. Or a twenty-seven.

Many golfers carry this card with them in a way that would have alarmed Joseph McCarthy. For them it is their license, their ticket, their identification in the muddy waters of a Thursday choose-up. Why not? The handicap locates us.

But let's face it: The handicap card is the three-dollar bill of the golf culture. Worthless. Inaccurate. Generally manipulated and abused. I'm not saying it couldn't work, this world where we stand in our mercerized cotton shirts and introduce ourselves as numbers. "I'm a twelve," I generally say. And you hear every number, every degree of pride and pshaw, when people discuss their handicaps. It should work, this system that allows the weak to play alongside the mighty, this grading curve that keeps men from fearing their own fallibility. The handicap card allows you to be just plain bad, to have a way to celebrate it. When placed in the right moment, in the right group, on the right course, the handicap can be a remarkable asset. But like many assets—pension funds, junk bonds, credit limits—it is abused. It makes us all charlatans, clowns, victims of one another's sloppiness and misunderstanding. The handicap card is not worth the adhesive that sticks it to its backing.

Spend one week watching the average game of golf, played by the average guy on a harmless course in a generally benign location, and you will begin to see what I mean. It may not be evident on a given day—the mulligan on the first hole, the reload where the out of bounds seemed too penal, the three kick-ins, the constant rolling of the ball in search of a real lie, the drop here and there. But over a week, over a month, over the course of twenty scores on his handicap card, it adds up. Weighty and absolute.

We all do it, save those who play with the purity of Tibetan monks. And like Tibetan monks, these guys are hard to find, fairly quiet and imbued with a sort of wisdom that is obscure to the rest of the world. They are unheard, ignored, and disrespected. The rest of us drop our cards in the boxes at our clubs, or enter them on untended computers in the corners of pro shops. Then we put the cheating behind us, get in our Buicks, and get on the interstate, our minds clear, our hearts still focused on one nine-iron shot where we stiffed the pin and snatched a skin for five lousy bucks. Those numbers, those scores, blend with other numbers, equally corrupt if only for a single penalty untaken, a single mulligan, to create this larger number, this measure of us as golfers, our handicaps, which purport to grade us to a tenth of a stroke. Why not take it down to a ten-thousandth of a stroke? "Hi, I'm Tom. I play at 12.3346." There would be an equal certainty that the number I'd give, the number anyone would give, would be a sort of rubber check. The lie remains the same. Worst of all, I'd be shaking your hand when I gave it to you.

Most golfers are cheats. We roll, kick, turnover, re-tee, and pickup. We get inside the leather without holing out, or reach inside the bag without thinking of the penalty. We permit transgressions from others in exchange for the same leniency for ourselves. In this way the game becomes like a prison yard, where strokes are traded like cigarettes and the guys who hold the most cigarettes run the joint.

So what of it? Why can't I lighten up and just recognize the obvious? Well, I'm telling you. I can. I do. I've learned to ignore handicaps, the way I ignore The Weather Channel. Those guys are always wrong. Always. In fact, they are right in only the broadest way possible. They don't grade the weather down to the nth decimal. They can't tell you which house will get hit by which tornado. In general, they are wrong. The storm arrives one county over. The lightning strikes where they least expect it. Wrong. Wrong. Wrong. But I still appreciate the effort.

I just decided to watch myself. I spent one week playing every day, taking every stroke, every penalty I knew of, and some only my opponents knew. Playing the wrong ball. Bing! Holing out with the flag in. Bam! Asking advice from an opponent. Wham! Walking off the stroke and distance, again and again. And I was stunned what it did to me, to my game, to my confidence and self-respect. My scores ballooned, two strokes a side at a minimum. Four, sometimes five, strokes a round, if not more. I was suddenly another man, a whole different handshake.

I did not consider myself much of a cheat. I know that I'm better than most about not giving myself breaks. But these things add up. By week's end, I had a pile of cards where the numbers were ugly, seriously so, and I kept them rubberbanded together in the glove compartment of my Buick. It was like carrying around a tumor.

Toward the end of that week, I was playing with a kid named Sam, the thirteen-year-old son of my ex-girlfriend. He has a beautiful swing and a mild temperament, and he closes in on me every time we play. On this Thursday, our bet was that when one of us lost the hole, the other would fake-cry all the way to the next tee box. Lose three-in-a-row and you would have to fake-weep. What can I say? The kid is seriously Christian and I just can't find pleasure scraping for money with a boy.

So we're on the ninth at my little club, an easy par-four, an iron out and a wedge in, the best birdie chance in the world for Sam. There is a semi-dangerous out-of-bounds area to the right, but nothing else to worry about. I crank my usual boring four-iron, and Sam steps up. He misses it dead right. Out of bounds.

"Maybe it got around the corner," I say, "but hit a provisional." So he re-tees without saying anything, and this one is worse. We laugh. He reloads. Three geese fly over. It is August and I haven't even thought of a goose in months. The year, I think, is twisting away once again. This time Sam blocks the ball enough so that it might be in play. Short of the corner, but in play.

"Better," I say, and Sam is a good sport, so he saddles up and we move with a smile.

But the ball is out—just out, like six inches past the white stake. Sam kicks it back in, tries to knock a four-iron under the trees, and goes out of bounds again.

In my head, I add it up: out of bounds four times, not calling a provisional aloud, one illegal drop. And now the cheats have piled up so high that I don't even know where to begin. The poor kid. I could tell him to pickup, but there's no one behind us.

He looks at me then. "How bad can this get?" he says.

"I don't know," I say. "But we might as well find out"

It is the only lesson worth learning to me these days. I want to add it up. Honestly. I want him to want it, too. I tell him to re-tee, to go back and walk it off. In the end, I'll write down a seven. But not until he holes out with a nineteen. Not until we both say the huge, improbable number and laugh about it.

In this way, just maybe, we'll give the game its due.

Strangers and Strange Lands

{ PART II }

(12) Pebble Beach

ON THIS THURSDAY, THE SUN SHINES A BRIGHT AND painful white on the skin of the Pacific. I stand on the tee of the eighth hole at Pebble Beach, thinking I deserve some measure of justice. My group jostles around me, turning to the sea, then back to the course, then to the sea again. Registering things. My caddy urges me to stay left. "Way left," he says, turning a toothpick in his mouth like a set screw for his brain. "Hit it so far left that you think you're hitting it off the course." We are blind to the flag. He points a finger, way left indeed, so that my target point appears to be ninety degrees from where I feel the ball should go. I feel confident, having just parred the notoriously short par-three seventh, with a nifty up and down, preceding that with two nice runs at birdies. But now there is a massive cliff in the distance, a nasty drop to the Pacific, one that I know about but cannot see from the tee. It's a good spot, puzzling what to do, playing into the best sequence of holes in golf. Eight, nine, ten at Pebble, figuring I've paid a lot of money, I've come a long way, and I've worked hard on my game. Figuring, in short, that I deserved it.

My caddy is an ex-fireman with the painfully plaintive name of John. My partners are three old guys from San Diego: a judge, a high school teacher, a realtor. Their names: Mike, Mike, and Jim. Their caddy: Ed. This is us, six guys with first names as ruddy and sensible as apples, walking the links at Pebble Beach, the greatest public course in the world, each of us eating up the experience, step by little step. We point, shake our heads, and—though we have only just met, me and them—we congratulate ourselves at the mere fact of being there. When the course takes its lurch toward the ocean, I feel that I am ready.

When you finish, when you go back to your little club and you let slip that you played Pebble Beach, your friends ask one thing: Was it worth it? They are referring to price, sure—the $350 round of golf, the eighty-dollar tip to the caddy, the three-dollar banana at the turn—but also to the effort of getting there, the difficulty of getting a tee time, the challenge of the course. But mostly they want to know about the journey. The one that every golfer takes. The one where you set yourself up against the game as a kid and you follow it to uncertain moments, toward an elusive pinnacle, the sense of arrival. If you're lucky, I suppose, this moment comes at Pebble Beach.

I have been playing golf fairly hard for seven years. In the seven years before that, I'd assumed I could play. In the seven before that, I only thought I could play. In the previous seven, I'd only wanted to play. Desire, followed by hope, then arrogance, then execution. The golfer lives his life in evolutionary segments. In each successive version of the golf-self, shorter for some, longer for others, he rises from the muck, upright in increments only, fish-to-man, back a little straighter, gait more steady. In the left-to-right of the familiar illustration, the golfer always assumes that he's made it to the Homo sapien edge of the chart, that he's the full golfer now, that his work has paid off. Then, when he fails—and he always fails—the golfer falls back on the idea of growth, capability, potential for more. Fish to man, always some measure of each.

So, there at the eighth, with the ocean only yards to the right, my caddy tells me to play my fade, to work the ball far to the left and let the wind carry it in. I'm on the back tee, thinking back to all the times I've seen this shot on television. Those guys take it to the very edge of the cliff; they dare themselves to face it. Aren't I ready? Can't I go right at it, gear down the swing, cut the driver just a bit to set myself up for the greatest second shot there is, over the cliff to the curvy salad bowl of a green?

My partners—the butcher, the baker, the candlestick maker—all hit irons from the front tee. Smart play. But from the back tee, I choose a driver. Isn't this it? Haven't I been waiting for this? Don't I deserve to knock this one ball to a firm and heady lie before I go stiff with some brave iron and knock the putt in from some reasonable distance? I do. I am visualizing. Seeing the moments ahead. I congratulate myself and choose a line. Left, the like the caddy said, but not that far left. Screw the caddie. He has no idea how ready I am.

In some ways, I'd been circling in on this moment for days, playing other, cheaper courses in the area. I'd banged around a nasty hill course called Laguna Seca in a miserable wind with two

Hispanic guys who hugged each other after good shots. Before that I'd grabbed a tee time at Pacific Grove, where I'd played the front nine with a guy named Ken and his wife, Ann, who were so old, so unsure of their footing, that they walked each other to the ball and held a hand on one another's back as they swung. The back nine at Pacific Grove swooshes by the ocean as grandly as any course in the world could hope to. I walked it with a beautiful woman named Anna who wasn't sure where to stand, how to address the ball, even how to carry her bag. She would drill it, then miss it; drill it, then miss again. She was there for a conference. But I was on top of things, eating up the back nine, going one under for the side with a birdie at eighteen. "You're ready for Pebble," she said in the parking lot. "I hope you play well." I felt that I might.

So it comes to moments like this, when you choose a driver when you shouldn't, when you cut your target line down a little too far, when you want it a little too much. There at the eighth at Pebble Beach, I crush the ball. At first the caddies like it, my ball rising hard and smooth to the left. Then the wind picks up, pushing the ball forward, toward the hole and toward the water all at once. We can see it take one huge bounce, and then we have to walk.

"It's a good line," says John.

"Maybe too much," says Ed.

"Maybe," says John.

Everyone seems to think it's fifty-fifty that the ball went over the cliff. It's the shot I wanted, I tell myself. I did what I was ready to do. As I approach the cliff, the ball is nowhere to be seen. As the old guys hit their second shots, which flair off, one-by-one, into the ocean, I search tall grass at the edge of the cliff for my ball. I should have hit the ball farther left, I tell myself, farther left than I could have ever imagined. John was right. The caddie generally is. I begin to see the fish in me. I had been incapable of imagining the shot. In that very inability, I had proven what I was.

There at the famous cliff, I can see the mundane fatness of the rest of the course, pressing out along the water toward the beach at Carmel, and I start to feel a sense that the experience is slipping away from me. People are swimming, snorkeling, lifting themselves on giant kites along the tops of the surf. The golf looks far less sacred in that moment, crammed belly-to-belly with all that recreation. And the end, I know, is near. After the twelfth Pebble takes its most pedestrian turn, and for three or four holes it feels like any other golf property, packed in alongside obscenely large houses. The caddies can tell you the selling prices of each. You even hear traffic. Not until the course returns to the ocean at the seventeenth green do you really pinch yourself again.

At the bottom of the cliff, some seventy feet below me, on a little scallop of sand, I see a couple sitting, facing the ocean. I look around, then yell down to them. "Hey," I said. "Did you see a ball come down there?"

They look up—two kids, arms around each other, tan, sunglassed, drinking beer from clear bottles—and laugh. "I heard something a couple of minutes ago," the guy says. "But I didn't see the ball."

I wave, kick the grass. "You have to lay up," the kid yells from below.

"I should have stayed left," I shout.

"You can't go far enough left," the kid says.

71

John the caddie shoulders up beside me, and the kid waves, then turns back to the water. "I couldn't make myself do it," I say. "I couldn't take it that far left."

John nods. "It's all right. That's just one shot."

"Yeah, but how many chances are you going to get to hit that shot? The eighth tee at Pebble. I thought I was ready."

John looks at the green, hands me a ball. "Then you're still ready. Look at this shot. It's the best shot in golf. It's sunny, too." He looks past me, at the horizon. "Man, look at the water."

He is right again. This is the shot, the one they show on television, across the ungodly cliffs, toward the heavily bunkered green. And the water, yes. I see it now. It's the color, the over-amped blue tight against the ferocious green. I get it.

So I drop, set up, and ease into a practice swing. Maybe this is why I came. Maybe this is what I was ready for all along. I've been building to this, I tell myself, to the only shot a golfer ever really deserves, the only one that matters. The next one, and all that come after.

13 Run, Sergio, Run

SERGIO GARCIA IS A MAN. OR HE IS A BOY. You can't be sure. The man wakes to do battle with other men. The boy wakes to grab a game or two on the Super Nintendo before heading off to practice. The man throttles Tiger Woods and plays him to the wire in the PGA. The boy finishes at thirty-two over par in the British Open and ends up weeping in his mother's arms. The man has a list of things he wants: to win a major championship, to crush his competition at every venue using every club in his bag, to be called Sergio, just Sergio, and nothing more. The boy appears to want for nothing, to be utterly happy playing a difficult game in a large field of grass with a stick in his hand. It's confusing. Only one thing is certain: Sergio Garcia wants to be your friend.

He's nineteen. Just months ago, he was the world's finest amateur golfer; now he's the world's most promising pro. It's all there, right in front of him. Everything he wants. His entourage knows it. His fellow players smell it on him. The crowds sense it. So he wades into galleries, signing, signing, signing. Golf balls. Hats. Programs. Photos. He writes his name on everything they hand him. Sergio, he writes again and again. Sergio, as if that explains it all. Fans rise and crackle in his presence. He high-fives children, grazes arms as he talks, rubs the occasional head for good luck.

During practice rounds, he flutters here and there, laughing, hanging on the other players like some kid brother to the whole world. But when Sergio reaches for a club, he transforms. His eyes narrow. His shoulders hitch, roll, then settle. He is another animal now, the one they're all betting on. This is not the ice-milk cool of David Duval or the pinched brow of Davis Love III or the put-upon pout of Tiger Woods; there's nothing painful in this expression. He comes out of his swing joyously, suddenly. He comes up smiling. This is Sergio, the boy who would be man.

Sergio wants to run. He's on the ninth hole at Carnoustie just before the 1999 British Open, grinding his way through a pretournament practice round. He's knocked down a five-iron from 210 yards. The wind blows lightly from the sea. In a few days, he'll melt down like a little boy and finish dead last at the cut, shooting a horrendous eighty-nine/eighty-three. But now he's drifting through the nasty lay-out like a seabird along the docks, nipping down now and again for a treat. He runs. It looks oddly natural to see a boy running down the middle of a fairway on a sunny day, but this one is flocked by chattering gaggles of children, who lift their legs in the high gorse, struggling to keep pace.

Later in the summer, he'll close his eyes and blast a six-iron from behind a tree at Medinah to within fifteen feet of the cup, a shot both marvelous and colossally stupid at the same time. He'll take off, breaking into a gallop, leaping into a childlike split in order to see the ball land gently on the distant green. "Sometimes I feel I have to run," he says. "Why not? It gives you a heartbeat." That he moves in contrast to the sometimes torpid and joyless pace of those around him, dashing straight into the cameras, is an accurate measure of who he is. He has always moved farther and faster than those around him, and the leap at Medinah is the moment that will define him here, at the doorway to his career.

Sergio is at the range, packed in cheek-by-jowl with the likes of tour veterans Larry Nelson, Steve Stricker, and Miguel Angel Jimenez. He strokes his four-iron crisply, each shot ten yards farther than the last—190, 200, 210. He maxes out at 260 yards, a massive shot by any standards, but no one seems to notice. It's as though he has been among them for decades.

Sergio is not imposing. He's reed-thin and narrow-waisted, slump-shouldered and lithe. He tippy-toes to five-feet-ten-inches and carries only 155 pounds on his frame. His face has that flushed, incomplete look of adolescence, making him appear trapped in the process of becoming, as if his bones were betraying him, growing to spite him. His smile, which he wears easily, is small, like a comma. You get the sense that another smile may exist beneath it, one that does not give in to modesty. He reminds you of someone. The kid who cuts your lawn. Your little brother. A skateboarder.

Sergio's swing reminds you of someone, too. Try Ben Hogan.

It's a free and oiled motion, powerful yet more contained than those of the tour's longest hitters. He whips through the ball, his hands low and sure, finishing the swing elegantly, hands high, elbows flexed. You could watch him hit a whiskey barrel full of range balls and never hear that familiar metallic clank that echoes on all sides of him. No, the sound of Sergio's impact is vicious and pure, as firm and reliable as the sound of a knife puncturing a melon. Each shot is a small assassination.

Sergio wants to be a man. He wonders aloud: "What is it to be a man? Can you take care of yourself? Can you watch your own way?" He puzzles a moment, weighing his life on the course—where he's been a man since he was hustling Cokes on the practice green at age six—against his life in the world—where he's surrounded by handlers, coaches, and managers.

The rituals, the rites of manhood, are a familiar drone. We circumcise, shave, tattoo, drive, deer hunt, lose our cherries. There's more than one line in the sand. For the golfer, coming of age is equally ambiguous. There are junior tournaments. Sergio took one of those before he was ten. There are club championships. He won his at twelve. There is making the cut in a pro event. He did that at fourteen. There's the amateur championship, which he won at fifteen. There is turning pro, which he did after being low amateur at the Masters Tournament last spring. Then he won in his sixth pro tournament, the Irish Open, and a month later finished second in the PGA.

Where were you at nineteen?

He's serious about this name business. The words tumble out, his English patchy and muscular all at once. "I like to be recognized as Sergio or Sergio Garcia," he says, "not as Garcia, just." After he pursued Tiger Woods at the PGA like a hacked-off bail bondsman, no one would dare call him Garcia, just.

He's been practicing press conferences since he was thirteen, and he trips into the clichés of sports whenever he's unsure of himself. "I think my mentality has always been a good one," he'll say. "But you never know what's going to happen. I now realize I can win some tournaments. And I'll try to do my best and keep playing well." These phrases, these lines, these reliable nuggets of nothingness, have been taught to him for protection. They are his armor, slipped over his slender shoulders by his teammates when he comes off the course. And make no mistake, Sergio has a team—a manager, an assistant, a tour-savvy caddie, a strength coach, and an English teacher. They refer to themselves as Team Sergio. Sergio refers to them as his family. *La familia.*

Among them, there is a breathlessness. They call down great things upon him, upon his career. At night, they eat together, and Sergio sits among them, a member of the team, part of the family. For them, it's been the better part of a decade in the making. For us, Sergio has only just begun.

His father and coach, Victor, club pro at Club de Campo del Mediterraneo in Borriol, Spain, learned the game by crafting his first set of shafts from olive branches, silently grooving his swing after sunset in his backyard. He came to know the swing better as a caddie, at a club where he was not allowed to play. Victor refuses to talk about Sergio. Instead, he trails his son during the rounds, always at a distance, but always recognizable for the yellow-shafted driver he carries tucked in the crook of his elbow like a regal weapon. He moves slowly and precisely, watching each move with an attitude approaching detachment. Still, it's obvious that his elegance, his calm, passes through to the boy. He is visible only to Sergio and bristles when the press pays him any mind. This man is no Earl Woods. There won't be any *Raising a Sergio* by Victor Garcia. He's there for the boy. "I'm glad he's there," Sergio the boy says. "I am learning from him, even when he's not talking. I need a father. Still. Always."

What Sergio doesn't want is to be compared to other phenoms, current or former. He wants no part of a comparison to Tiger Woods, though he wouldn't mind a rivalry. "I have my own swing, my own game. I am Sergio. Just me," he says.

Woods smiles wryly when asked about Sergio. "When you get off to a good start at a young age, you're very confident. You're vivacious. You feel like you can play well against anybody at any time. That's what he was able to do when he turned pro," Woods says. Then he cools. "As far as a rivalry, I don't think there is one. Yet."

When Woods, twenty-three, bagged his second Majors at Medinah in August 1999, the television guys rolled out the inevitable graphics, comparing his first three years on tour with Jack Nicklaus's. We need these yardsticks in sports. They press the now flush against the then, forcing us into parallels where there were none before. One thing was clear that Sunday: If Tiger is indeed the next Jack Nicklaus—the stern, corporate taskmaster, the ultimate measuring stick—then Sergio can be the next Arnold Palmer, the guy with the legion of fans, chasing the favorite, glaring from green to tee, taking brave chances, and drawing us toward him as he invents victory again and again.

Back at Carnoustie, in the weeks before his emergence into the larger golf consciousness, Sergio is surrounded during a practice round. There are enough fresh-faced British schoolboys in the crowd to stage a revival of *Oliver*, and they all seem to have scented Sergio, to have marked him as one of their own. Their fathers follow close behind, picking up hints, rules to live by.

When Sergio stops to putt, they talk. "Look at his hands," one of the fathers whispers, nudging his boy. When the putt drops, Sergio runs again.

"Where's he going then?" asks one of the boys

"Just look at him," his father says. "Amazing."

Silent and stock-still, they watch him. Sergio's off to the next tee box, then onward. Just going. The wind is freshening, but for a moment the crowd hangs back. Sergio grows smaller in the distance. They know where he's going. They know that he'll get there. And they follow him, man and boy alike.

(14) Blown Away

I HAVE A SEVEN-IRON IN MIND. I'M THINKING OF A HIGH, drifting shot from about 145 yards out, landing on the front edge of the green, curling toward the cup. It's the sort of shot you might picture eight or nine times in a given round. The bread and butter of shot visualization. But as it happens, I'm on the 398-yard third hole at Panmure Golf Club, in Barry, in the County of Angus, about a mile from the Tay, along the east coast of Scotland, and the problem is the wind is blowing so hard that my eyes are watering nonstop. The gusts create a sound like someone rubbing a nylon tent in my ear. From the tee, I hit my driver straight into the howl, which lifts the ball absurdly high into the air, holds it there for a laugh, and drops it in the short grass like a dead bird. I follow with a one-iron into the teeth of the wind, and the ball collapses right-ward into a half-moon shot to the next fairway, advancing nowhere. From there, I band another one-iron, which humps along the fairway awkwardly. Now I'm 145 yards out, and I have a seven-iron in mind.

From across the fairway my host is yelling at me, but I can't hear a word. He's a Scot to the core, a stock-thick, iron-armed cat named Iain Anderson. He drove here on a 1950 Vincent motorcycle at eighty miles an hour, leaning hard into every curve, while I poked along behind him, clinging to the left side of the road in a rented Rover, lugging his loaner clubs for our match by the sea. Yesterday, I watched him effortlessly hold up the back end of the motorcycle with one hand for fifteen seconds to slide out and replace a grease sheet. He is sixty-five. His hair long and driven white, he looks like a conceptual drawing of a Scotsman.

Even in the parking lot, the wind thrust toward us. "This is quite normal," he said before pulling his hat on with two hands. "You'll have to get used to it."

But now I can't hear what he's saying. Something about a pearl. Or a whirl. I wave and I can see him laughing, but the wind is blowing so hard I have the distinct sensation that he's in another place, on another hole, in another room. I squint and turn an ear. What's he saying? Give it a whirl? Don't twirl? I wave.

Scotland is hard. Hard as in difficult, tough, resilient. Hard as in a diamond. Hard as in unbreakable. It's no secret that golf was born here. But Scotland's inventions are likely more elemental than that. Wind was born here, too, I'm sure. And grass—real grass, bud, waist-high and sticky with its own scaly skin—was born here, too. Clouds, too, maybe.

Iain has lent me a set of ancient, bone-dry Hogans, a shabby collection of irons, and a pocketful of shag balls. The grips on these clubs are dusty with their own crumblings. The balls are cut with grim Scottish smiles. Iain snorted when I tried to buy a sleeve at the shop. "Ye won't be needing a new ball," he said. "Not here. Not anytime soon." We ate steak-and-onion sandwiches at the bar before we played. Mine was tough and tasteless. I pulled it apart with my teeth while I watched the flags snapping rigidly in the midday wind. Three men played cards at the table next to us. One of them hated his hand and threw it down, hissing, "That's a pile of pants!" as if there could be nothing more worthless.

I think about yelling to Iain, there on the third—me with my seven-iron in hand, him shouting about pearls, holding his hat down on his head—that this is a pile of pants. I have on three shirts—in July—and face seven more holes straight into the wind before we are to turn back downwind for the finish. Lying three, dead into the gale, holding a bag of clubs that wouldn't fetch a sawbuck at a garage sale, with my host yelling at me indecipherably—if ever there were a pile of pants, this is it.

I address the ball, curling my ear against my shoulder to keep the wind from blowing right through me. I can hear Iain now. "Girl!" He's been calling me a little girl. He repeats it.

"This isn't Florida, Turn. Ye kant bee a wee girl! Just hit it."

A girl. The guy is calling me a girl. If there's ever been a time I wanted to get snug against the flag, this is it. I have to get there. I'll hit it straight through the green even. I grab the two-iron, roll it in my hands, and make a quick address. Strangely, I know this is the right club—a two-iron from 145 yards—but I cannot picture the shot.

The truth is, it's hard to visualize anything when you're standing on this particular facet of the golf planet. You have to have imagination. I'm not talking about thinking outside of the box. These guys don't give a good goddamn about the box. You have to think big.

Golfers talk about imagination all the time: hitting off the hard pan to an elevated green, flying the bunker to a four-foot patch of green, hammering a long, low draw around a stand of palm trees. All golfers must learn to be able to see and do things they've never done. That's why I think it's a better game than, say, tennis, in which you are forced to see yourself endlessly doing the same thing. Backhand, backhand, backhand, crosscourt forehand, go pick up your ball.

But it's hard to imagine a well-hit two-iron not going far more than 145 yards. Maybe you've missed it like that once. Sure you have. But getting your head clear on doing it intentionally takes some doing. For me, it's normally a 210-yard shot, maybe more. Trimming it to 145, giving it the extra loft, dealing with the gusts and the near-by gorse, heather, and sea grass—this is like trying to park a Hummer at a strip mall; it can be done, but it'll take some circling.

Smooth two. That's my swing thought. To my left, sheep bleat. An RAF plane loops home to the nearby base. It's Scotland, where the land—every bit of it, every sound, every wisp, every taste, every drop of mist, every word uttered into the deafening wind—pushes you closer to the game than you have ever been. You want to have your game in Scotland. You need to. I reach back, drawing on my reserves, hooding the club, lowering the takeaway, shortening the follow-through. Good thing, too, because I meet the ball on the screws, and I think: That's it. That'll show him.

This ball, unlike others I've hit dead upwind, wobbles a bit, then finds its legs and bears down on the hole. It thumps down ten yards in front of the green and hops into a roll before settling at the back edge. I've hit a true knockdown off a full swing, not some bogus half-iron. It's the essence of Scottish golf, which demands imagining the interplay of wind, rolling heath, and the spasms of your ball flight. It is a mean, hard, leveling game.

When I catch up with Iain, he's proud of me. "Fine shot, Turn. Ye hit it like a golfer there," he says.

We're shoulder to shoulder. I can hear him just fine now. The wind whistles. "I left myself a long putt," I say.

He pauses and takes a look at the green. "Aye, but the putt is downwind." We press on. There's a storm in front of us and sunshine at our heels. A downwind putt. Good God. I'm walking now, trying hard to see the possibilities before me.

15 Golfing the Cherry

DON CHERRY STANDS IN A DOORWAY, ONE FOOT in, one foot out of his Las Vegas ranch house. He's tapping his toe, fidgeting in the pockets of his windsuit. The sun shines. His golf cart is loaded. We're waiting on his wife. He rocks on his heels. Outside, then in again. He wants to get going.

The doorway between one world and another seems the perfect spot to take a snapshot of this man who has lived a life with his feet firmly planted in two spheres: golf and entertainment. In some ways, he is the man every golfer wants to be, which is to say he is an entertainer, a crooner of the first order who hobnobbed with the Rat Pack and sang his way to a gold record. In other ways, he is the man every crooner wants to be, which is to say he is a golfer with a first-class record who hobnobbed with some of the great personalities of the game, among them Jimmy Demaret and Tommy Bolt. He's the golfer who knocked 'em dead in the lounge at the Desert Inn for years, who

Vic Damone dubbed the "singer's singer," who ran with Dean Martin and Buddy Hackett from one high-profile gig to another throughout the '60s and '70s. But he's also the singer who happened to be undefeated in Walker Cup play, who played in the Masters nine times as an amateur, who played himself to within one shot of the lead with two holes to play in the 1961 U.S. Open at Cherry Hills.

Looking at Cherry now, it's hard not hard to see both versions of him. At seventy-eight, he's at home on a golf course; he isn't as long as he once was, but he knocks the balls as straight as the noonday sun and he putts like a champ. When he sings, and he does so throughout the round, his voice fills up every empty space, as resonant and rich as a thunderstorm. He golfs better than most men sing, but the truth is, even now he sings better than, well, just about anybody.

So why don't more people know him as one or the other? I ask Cherry and he growls a little. It's a question he's been asked a thousand times before. "I made choices. I could always play golf and I could always sing. For a long time, one complemented the other. I loved them both; I just never gave up one for the other. I didn't feel I had to."

So now, at the age when most men are considering giving up golf, Cherry is considering his next gig, his next CD, and his next benefit concert, all the while editing the final draft of his memoir: *Cherry's Jubilee: I Never Played the Game.*

The subtitle is puzzling since Cherry did play the game and he did it very well. Raised by a single mother, Cherry "came up" as a player in what was generally considered to be the breadbasket of golf in the '40s and '50s, West Texas, in the tiny town of Wichita Falls to be precise. The game came easily to him, and his mother, who made her money as a seamstress and lived her life through a strong connection to the Church of Christ, didn't stand in his way, so long as he sang. "When I was little, she wanted me singing," Cherry says. "It's all I can remember. Me at six or seven years old, wondering why people were staring at me while I sang. I'd ask my mother and she'd say, 'They're staring because they know how good you are.'" Cherry rubs his chin. "She was a tough woman, so I kept singing and I never stopped."

As he grew Cherry nursed both talents. In the years after the war, he racked up amateur golf championships like it was nobody's business but his, totaling fourteen in nine years Throughout the '50s, he played in top-level competitions, befriending a number of golfers, such as three-time Masters Champion Jimmy Demaret, who loved Cherry's game but truly worshipped his singing voice. More important, Demaret was a friend and supporter to Cherry throughout the '50s, when Cherry was cutting his teeth in major competitions while singing in lounges at night. "He was what my father should have been," Cherry said. "He really took care of me." By 1961, the year he turned pro, Cherry had compiled the only undefeated record in the history of Walker Cup play. To this day, his 5-0 record in singles and foursome play remains a Walker Cup standard.

As a golfer, Cherry was known as a guy who bent clubs and tossed bags as often as, or more often than, he won. As with his two primary talents, his anger seemed like a gift at birth, one he was unable to deny. "I'll tell you when I figured out I was a hothead," Cherry says as we sit just outside his kitchen sipping bottled water. "When I was less than ten years old, I used to caddy for my brother on the halves, and they played a dime a hole. One day he's playing against three other guys and he comes to the last hole and, with the presses and all, he's up

130 dimes. Thirteen dollars! And I'm going to get half. So he hit it right down the middle on eighteen. Then he choked a wedge and rolled it in the water. Right then I took the bag, walked to the pond, and gently laid it in the water. I dropped his clubs right on top of his ball. That's when I knew what I was. Wasn't even ten years old."

Throughout his amateur career, Cherry held a reputation for this temper. It wasn't until he moved to New York to pursue his singing that he learned to cool down. "They didn't know me," he says. "They didn't have to put up with me." Still, he is sanguine about his temper and its effect upon his life, seeing it as more of a phase than a character flaw. "Every friend I had was a friend. I never lost anyone because of my temper. Now I'm at the point where I can't understand when someone hits the ground after a shot. Total turnaround, I guess, but the truth is I just gave up on anger."

The question persists: What if Cherry had made that kind of simple choice in his career path—golf or music? Would he have made that final small step from the merely excellent—the top-ranked amateur, the reliable studio artist—to the immortal—a major champion or music icon? By all accounts, the step was not a large one in either area. The amateur record shows he had the tools to dominate. As for the singing, "Dean Martin once told me that I could fart better than Frank Sinatra sang," Cherry laughs. "But I'm pretty sure he didn't mean it."

One thing is certain: He didn't lose anything in either of his careers to drinking or smoking. Cherry has never had a drink in his life, though that never deterred him from hanging out with people who did. "The four best friends I ever had—Mickey Mantle, Bobby Lane, Phil Harris, and Dean Martin—were the four biggest drunks who ever walked. I loved every one of them. I just never dove in. Dean would have done anything to get me to drink. He once offered me five hundred dollars to drink a pineapple daiquiri. I looked at him and said, 'It's not going to happen.' You can pretty much stand up to anyone after him." As for not smoking, he says, "That was all about my mother. She just wouldn't have it, so I never got started."

Still, in the starched-collar era of the '50s, Cherry's night-and-day contrast was too much for many of the most powerful men in golf. During the '54 Masters, Cherry took a job singing in a night-club during the tournament. After the second day, Cherry was called into Cliff Roberts's office. "We're pleased you're here," Roberts said, "but I have to tell you that we've never had anyone play in the Masters and sing at a nightclub."

"Mr. Roberts, I've seen the list," Cherry deadpanned, "and I don't see anyone on there who can sing."

Later on, an aging Bobby Jones called him aside, waving him over with his cigarette holder. "Donald," he said, "that's a great answer you gave Mr. Roberts. Do me a favor and don't ever give it again."

His success as a vocalist and as an amateur champion reached its peak in 1961 at the U.S. Open at Cherry Hills, where Cherry found himself in a group of five players within one stroke of eventual champion Arnold Palmer. Cherry had given Palmer a terrific chase in 1954 for the U.S. Amateur, and now he was poised for revenge. "I ran in a forty-footer for birdie on fourteen, and Sam Snead said 'You're going to win the tournament.' And I thought, 'Oh, Lord.'" The jinx was on, and Cherry missed birdie putts on fifteen and sixteen, then took a seven on eighteen to finish in a tie for seventh.

The next year, Cherry turned pro. He never duplicated his amateur success, probably because his singing career really started taking off. For ten years, Cherry was probably most widely heard as the voice of "Mr. Clean" on television commercials. He made nearly $800,000 during that decade simply from that single voiceover job. Throughout the '60s and '70s, television appearances racked up—*The Dean Martin Show*, the shows of Arthur Godfrey and Merv Griffin, and later *Hee Haw* and *Nashville Now*—and the hit songs—"Band of Gold," "Take a Message to Mary," "Wild Cherry"—strung themselves into a reliable fan base that allowed him to headline larger venues. Cherry often booked himself to sing on the weekend of a tournament. "That made it so I knew I had money coming, no matter where I was," he says as we walk to his golf cart for the short ride to the first tee.

Cherry is an honest guy, admirably so. You can hear the paradoxical mixture of pride and regret in almost everything he says. The past may bother him, but he's not reliving his choices, and he is not loath to admit that the music may have hurt his game as a pro. "I know it took its toll. It had to, but I got fulfillment from both things. I'm never sorry for either one."

By late afternoon, we find ourselves waiting on the fifteenth hole for a group ahead of us. Cherry takes a deep sigh and looks like he's had enough of golf. He's just returned from a benefit to raise money for a memorial for his son, who died in the attack on the World Trade Center. Soon he'll be appearing with Willie Nelson as part of a fundraiser for Ladybird Johnson. He's got to be tired.

"It's just been a hell of a year. Losing Stephen in one day. Watching it all on television," he says. "Man, I guess I was like everyone else. There I was in my bedroom in Las Vegas, watching all this stuff happen half a world away. I was afraid to admit that any of it was happening." I can see that it hurts him to have been so far away yet so near during the massacre, caught between two worlds once again.

On the next hole, I can see that his spirits are lifting. He wants to get home and change for the photo shoot we're planning that afternoon. He's let me pick the suit, a classy Versace number, and we're setting him up at sundown on the first green. The lounge singer oddly in his element on the golf course. I ask him if he's going to sing while we shoot the pictures and he laughs. "You bet I will."

Then I ask him if he'll sing something from the new CD, his tribute to Perry Como. Cherry mistakes it for a request and before I know it he's singing "Without a Song."

At first, the mixture is jarring, one voice in all the emptiness, one man singing against the Nevada wind. But within seconds he has filled the air. When he stops after one verse, I ask him to go on. And so he sings as we play the hole, and with each step we take I can feel the two worlds—the song and the game, the man and the past—pulling together. I urge him all the way through the song, and by the end we're both laughing at the ludicrous contrast, the beautiful song of loss paired against two long putts in a meaningless game. Cherry's song is, I can say with certainty, the most incredible thing I've ever heard on a golf course. I'm too astounded to even clap.

"I suppose," I say, "if I was a woman, I'd be in love with you now."

Cherry laughs. "Yeah," he says as he putts out, "the good part is, sometimes it works out that way."

16　My Brother's Greenskeeper

LIFE DOESN'T PRESENT MANY PRECIOUS moments on a golf course. Most often, you take your lickings, settle your bets, and then order a club sandwich. Be grateful when appropriate, sure. You can thank a friend for inviting you to the member-guest, but that's about all the emotion you need. Bring your A-game, bet yourself in the Calcutta, but leave the sincerity in the car.

Now cut to the eleventh green at the Revere at Anthem, outside Las Vegas, where my brother Frank, stocky as a soup can, hungover, and missing his sunglasses, has just flopped a shot from a thin lie to within four feet. He holds out his arms as I come on the green. "Nice shot," I say. I'm twenty feet from the cup, staring down a makable birdie.

On the next tee box, a guy sits on a mower, waiting for us to finish up. The sun is somewhere nearby, lighting the world so fully that it appears to have leaked into every corner, eliminating the question of shadow. It's stone-quiet—which is to say I can hear a mower or two, the distant pulse of the interstate, a dry breeze across my ear. My brother's arms are still out.

It is 12:06 P.M. We are in the desert, on a small, sloping green, next to a masonry wall, behind an unfinished house where a contractor is even now frantically shoveling Dryvit into a wheelbarrow. Cars prowl the canyon road above us. We are a couple dozen miles from our hotel, two time zones from our families, and a mere six hours off the craps tables, drinking ten-dollar Bloody Marys from the drink cart and bearing down on each other—auto-pressing, air-pressing, re-pressing on the one-dollar basic bet. We're in it about seventeen ways, standing in the middle of nowhere with no tangible reason to connect with anything in the world we know, and my brother wants a hug.

The next time you glide westward on a Whisperliner, just as you're hanging over the desert take a look out the window. You'll find your basic expanse, gritty and edged by mountains, with the occasional ribbon of highway, cushioned by the glint of one desert town or another. Every now and then, dropped like some glob of fluorescent paint at the base of the hills—a golf course. There. And there, too. From the air, they beckon like roadside attractions, asking that you pause and contemplate, if only for a moment, setting the whole rig down right there.

From the air, desert golf courses look like scabs, like tiny wounds on the skin of the sand. Barstow, Mesquite, Wendover—these places hurt! Even the towns are wounds. But land is cheap in the desert, or it was once, and technology barrels forward. Golf courses unfold again and again in the least green of the scorched earth. They gather and multiply around the greatest desert scab of all, the scab that works: Las Vegas. They knew I would show up eventually.

Brothers do this. They fly off to Vegas to play golf, to a spot both crowded and lonely at once, familiar yet insulated from everything that is likewise familiar. Playing golf anywhere is like that. You slink away to the edge of your world for some communion. You deal with time and partnerships, with money and age. You nail a few pars, string together a few moments. As with Vegas itself, you leave the golf course excited, drained, ready to have at it again soon. In Vegas, brothers stretch that out—hanging in hotel restaurants, ordering eggs, talking about their children, about the places they hide money, and about the dark-ass bar where one of them saw an old friend drinking at two in the afternoon. They call each other names. They take walks to see the fish tank at the Mirage. They wish Don Rickles were in town. They grab tee times when they can get them and head to the desert each morning, parched already, worn out and gritty from the night before, gamely fighting the sassiest, sweetest battle of them all—a round of golf with your brother.

Playing golf with your brother is like watching yourself on a store surveillance camera's tape. The guy you're looking at could be you, or maybe not. The moves are the same, even the clothes. Same big head, same hitch in the shoulders. His swing has the same over-tight lunge, and, like you, he can hammer the ball once in a while. But it's all a bit foreign and vaguely embarrassing, watching yourself in the swing of a brother.

So my brother and I try not to watch each other. We never offer advice. We hit and move. We sit in the cart and hold our icy drinks against our foreheads. We talk. We need to talk. On the course, we can go seven holes without talking about anything but the clubs in our bags, the price of real estate, and the importance of really good bacon. We try each other's drivers.

At the fifth hole, he asks me why he never got the DVD player I ordered him for Christmas. Two holes later, I drill a three-iron to within a yard of the flag and say, without realizing I had been thinking about it for twenty years, "Why did you let that little bastard Finn borrow Dad's car? Didn't you know better?" Damned if I can remember what he said. Minutes later, we were on to penny stocks and protein diets, to architects and football teams, happy to have two more days yawning ahead of us. Two days to talk about nothing whatsoever. About everything in particular.

That very morning, I sat on the edge of my bed and told Frank I didn't think I could make it. Something was wrong with me. No energy. Twelve hours at the craps table, forty minutes of sleep. I didn't feel that I could put on my own shoes. I shook my head. "I feel bad," I said. "I'm not sure I can make it."

"You'll be okay," he said. "Come on."

Easy for him to say. He'd slept for two hours.

I stood. Then sat. Then put my head on the pillow. Frank grabbed my chin and stared me in the eye. "You need pancakes," he said. "Pancakes will take care of this."

"I don't know," I said, closing my eyes.

He kicked the bed. "Come on," he said. "Get up. We'll talk.

You just need to talk a little."

I knew he was right. I could still rally. So I rose. I had to. I was there to play golf, the talker's game.

Later that afternoon, when I grab Frank for his hug I jostle him a little, assuming the hug will be a kind of glorified chest bump. But Frank holds on. "Nice shot," I say again, still assuming that he's pleased about the flop shot, which was no small trick, given that shitty lie. He holds on even longer, and I start to laugh. The guy on the mower gears down his engine. My putt is still there. Frank's got a gimme. No wonder he's so damned happy. "Frankie," I say, his name the purest assertion of the moment. But he holds on. Pretty soon I grab on and we're both laughing, half drunk in the full light of everything, in the most private public space there is—on the golf course, in the desert, at the edge of the world. At that very moment, I'm sure people are flying over us, looking down at all of this, saying to themselves: "Look at that, another golf course! Won't they ever have enough?"

Frank's not talking now, though. He's not letting go, either. He doesn't say much more than: "Thanks for this." He doesn't need to. I know exactly what he's saying, and I have plenty more to tell him.

17 The Last Great Golf Course

IN ARCHITECTURE, MANY CONNECTIONS ARE CALLED moments. The column meets a beam. That's a moment. The roofline meets its peak. Another moment. When my brother Frank was an architecture student, we stood in a parking garage in Salt Lake City and he told me, "To get my license, I'd have to be capable of calculating every moment in this whole place."

I looked around. "How many moments is that?"

His eyes went wide. "Hundreds," he said. "Maybe thousands."

Since then, it's been hard for me to see most average human structures as anything other than massive skeletons of stress points. The shopping mall. The highway overpass. My dentist's office. One moment after another, one indistinguishable from the next. Even the average golf course, where the premium would seem to always be on architecture and design, seems a mere string of calculations to me—sculpted rise, gentle berm, scalloped edges of the pond. The

97

same mind-numbing visual language from one course to another.

But then there are the great courses—Augusta, Pine Valley, Pinehurst No. 2, Pebble Beach, Sand Hills—each of which can be said to be singular and complete, a thousand decisions nestled inside one vision. On these courses, the level of calculation is a daily puzzle, one that takes a lifetime to sort out. Great courses are a moment unto themselves. As the great course falls into place, word gets out before it is even played. Right now, the word is that it's happening in a little town in Oregon called Bandon, at a public course called Pacific Dunes, which opens this July. This is a moment that will begin there and then. It may be the last of its kind.

Cliché dictates that the world is shrinking. In the matter of golf courses, this is surely so; the era of the great course is at a close. There isn't enough suitable land left in the United States. Developers are properly hamstrung by land-use restrictions, environmental protections, zoning boards. Nor is there enough patience, or talent, or taste, to build them the way they ought to be built. Or money. Not to mention balls. You have to have some large measure of each to build a great golf course.

Even as the fairways grow into their contours, even as the greens grab hold of the sand, even before anyone pays a penny to play it, Pacific Dunes looks ancient, as though it's been there all along. It looks as though someone picked up the rug and found a golf course, a course confidently featuring the four pillars of greatness—ocean, vegetation, contour, and wind—without relying too much on any one of them.

Pacific Dunes sits along a twenty-three-mile stretch of undisturbed Oregon coast, atop hundred-foot cliffs, in and amongst a tangle of gorse, sea grass, and sand dunes. This is the sort of place you'd stand for a look at the world—the dense blue ocean, the heaving surf, the whales, the crab boats, the distant points of sand and rock. It is a place both remote and connected, both distant and familiar, where nature and man press on in their various forms of commerce and decay.

You have to picture this land, beaten upon by the surf and the wind, a small river dragging sand to the ocean, the tides heaving it back up into mountainous dunes, which the Coos and Coquille tribes used for centuries as a meeting ground. When the loggers came, a homesick Irishman shipped in several gorse bushes to give the area an Irish flavor. The gorse, far from the cold and bitter soil of the British Isles, where it grows in low clumps, exploded, overtaking everything for sixty miles along the Oregon coast until the area became a forest of the stuff, twenty feet deep in places, as dark and thorny as any medieval fairy tale.

Being able to build here at all at this juncture in history was a matter of patience and luck—that of owner Mike Keiser, who set out to build a great course and nothing less. He started looking in the late eighties, bought the Bandon property five years later, and took three years to get all the permits, variances, and trust needed to break ground. Keiser was in no particular rush. "Every time you start a course like Pacific, you have a chance to build a cathedral, something that will outlast us all. There's no reason to rush. Plus, we literally couldn't walk the land, it was so deep in the gorse."

Things fell together. The strong economy. The decade-long golf boom. The peculiarities of land-use restrictions for the Oregon coastline. The surprising assent of the Indian tribes (who see the land as largely undisturbed by the low-impact design of Pacific Dunes). The demise of logging and fishing in the area (providing a town hungry for new jobs). Even the locals' hatred of the uncontrollable gorse. These were the X factors that allowed Pacific Dunes to move forward. But the catalyst was a brush fire that consumed four hundred acres of gorseland in late 1999, allowing Keiser and course designer Tom Doak their first real look at the lay of the land.

"The gorse was so deep you literally couldn't see anything, before the fire," said Keiser. "And then, suddenly, there was this golf course right in front of us."

Building the golf course that was presented to them fit the aesthetic of Doak, who disdains heavy equipment and earth moving. He's a smallish guy, infamously demanding in the matter of course design, who both walks the course and plays it in the same pair of ratty work boots. As we play the course, his first time playing all eighteen holes in order, Doak points with pride to the places he didn't work on and apologizes for those places he did. Again and again, he passes a delicate green site without comment, moving straight to an untouched dune, which he seems to know so intimately it might have a name.

"It's great moving the world around," he says, studying a thirty-foot ridge of sand replete with the stubble of sea grass. "But all the equipment in the world couldn't do this."

We're standing at the thirteenth, facing the ocean, playing slowly through the holes at Pacific Dunes. When I ask Doak about making his mark on the game, he won't bite. But when asked if the course will last, he is firm.

"There are seven holes which run directly into or along the shoreline in some way," he says. "Those are hundred-foot cliffs. I know there are greens which will fall into the water eventually. That's happened at some of the Irish courses, like Ballybunion. But the truth is, that kind of thing will be a lot of fun to deal with in a hundred years."

This, too, is a kind of connection, a moment, this architect speaking to another architect about this one place a hundred years from now. The new hole suddenly seems, as great holes do, both intentional and accidental, as broad and permanent as the continent itself. To the west, the surf works the shore. To the east, a band of workers quietly pulls burnt stumps of gorse from the deep rough by hand. Doak tees up. The wind picks up from the north. There is no hint of a different past, of a time when the hole wasn't there, except for what I can read in the reaction of the workers, who crane their necks. Doak is the first guy they've seen playing the hole. They want a look. They want the moment to last.

18 The Troubles

I'M DRIVING THE RING OF KERRY WITH THREE GUYS named Sullivan. Just the four of us, on this notoriously winding mountain road in southwest Ireland, fresh off an eight-hour Aer Lingus flight, two hours in our shitty rental Renault, pressed in cheek-by-jowl one against the other, heading to our first stop—a golf course, like every stop planned for the week—the Ring of Kerry Golf and Country Club. It's raining. Nasty, cold, sideways-blowing rain. No weather for golf, none whatsoever. More like weather for chess. Weather for fireplaces. Weather for television and pretzels. Wipers slapping this way, then that, nary a word passes among us as we careen along the ridgelines, plunge down the slick and narrow mountain roads. At one point, we come to a clutch of driveways where the road is full of massive cows being herded toward a milk shed, forcing us to a dead stop. It is a cliché in the making, four golfers held steady against the ancient commerce of the herdsman. The third Sullivan, who is driving today, takes out his camera just as the road starts to clear, snapping a picture through the windshield.

"Why don't you roll down the window?" the first Sullivan says. "That picture won't come out."

The third Sullivan inches the car forward. "We have a tee time," he says. "We need to get there so we can hit some balls first." In front of us, a Border collie bites hard on the leg of a large white cow.

On a sustained Irish golf trip, moments of rest are spent thumbing through tourist brochures for a sense of where the nearest driving range might be. You wake up only to drive to the next course, ninety minutes or more along the hedgerows, between and around the tiny lorries with their loads of tin, their crates of eggs. You play with three guys you know only sort of glancingly from your little club. At the end of the day—wet, mud-spattered, blistered, windburned, and dry-mouthed—you return to distant bed-and-breakfasts, where you eat your meals and recount the shots and drink your drinks, only to sleep, then rise to do it again.

Don't mistake this for anything but what it is—hardcore golf, not tourism. It is a kind of training, an indulgent discipline, wrought on golf courses as confounding as they are elegant. This is the sort of trip sure to sicken the traveler who dog-ears guidebooks. No museums. No boat rides. No tours of cathedrals. Day after day, the sun rises, the television news drones on, the traffic trudges this way and that, and you play golf. Each day is like the last, except in matters of tee-box alignment and crosswinds and depth of heather. There is scenery, to be sure—slate-gray sea; vast, deserted beaches; hoary sand dunes sunbaked and spiked with grass. Irish golf courses are beautiful in the same manner that farms are beautiful; a sense of care is evident, but every aspect of their appearance and practice represents labor. Hard labor, too—not for the greenskeeper so much as for the golfer. Playing them doesn't require calculation so much as commitment.

If you want to get better, to finally raise your game to the next level, find ten days in your life, locate three golfers, fly to Ireland, set the stakes, and play. You will get your butt kicked by something—the courses, the weather, the grass, the wind. These moments will force you to pull yourself together, to face up to it when a course is beating you over and over again. Do not stop. Do not quit.

At Waterville, the brutal links course at the very end of County Kerry's Iveragh Peninsula, we set out at 7:00 A.M. in a driving rain. The holes throb with heather, and the ocean hisses like a big, indifferent ghoul in the distance. The three Sullivans and I stand at the clubhouse pawing through our bags for earmuffs and plastic bag covers like women rooting in their purses for tampons. Then we head out, straight into the heart of it. At the end of the ninth hole, we find a statue wrapped completely in garbage bags. I point to the giant man, covered in flapping plastic, as we limp in for a cup of tea at the turn.

"What do you think that's about?"

"It's raining," the first Sullivan says. "I bet it's supposed to be a raincoat."

"They're garbage bags," the second Sullivan replies.

The first Sullivan reasserts himself. "I'm telling you, they want you to wear a raincoat. They're telling you to wear a coat. That's the Irish way. They are very considerate."

At this point, it has been raining for thirty-six hours without cease; the other Sullivans won't have it. They don't want to hear theories. They point to the first Sullivan's ball, resting near a puddle at the base of a sand dune.

"What do you lie?" they ask him. The wind picks up. The garbage bags flap in the wind. The next day, on the way to Ballybunion, we read in the paper that the as-yet-to-be-unveiled statue is a likeness of Payne Stewart, the honorary captain at Waterville. "You see?" says the first Sullivan. "I told you they were considerate."

At Ballybunion, we play the new course, a Robert Trent Jones nightmare, into the teeth of a wind that pours off the ocean, cold and foul. The course is all carry, all test and trial, and the caddie master assigns us two bony junior caddies who, instead of watching our shots, shield their eyes against the needlepoints of rain from the shore. I'm determined to get off to a good start, but by the third hole I'm nine over par and thinking about walking off. There is soup at the bar, and there are newspapers there, and there's a telephone booth where I can go to call my family. But the third Sullivan is in worse shape than I, having taken a ten on the first hole, and the course is about to take a sudden, notable lurch toward the sea.

Off the fourth tee, I hit a solid three-wood, which jump-slides into the heather about 220 yards out. In the deep grass, it takes me a full five minutes to find the ball, which I mark by leaving a hat next to it before turning back to get a club. The Sullivans stand at various points, in the fairway and off, lining up shots. When I return to the grass, I cannot find the hat. The clouds seem to have dropped down on top of us now. I check my line, look for a landmark, and start in again. No luck. While the two caddies help me, the Sullivans hit away. We descend the small hill and poke around in the grass until I am soaked to midthigh. The hat and the ball are absolutely gone into the texture of the rolls of tall grass and sand. Having lost a ball, a hat, and the hole in one moment, I cannot make myself walk back to the tee, so I concede the hole and drop a ball. I bear down, punch a four-iron, and two-putt for an ersatz double bogey. Not all that bad when you consider the first Sullivan takes a seven after losing two shots in the heather, the second Sullivan cards a par, and the third Sullivan picks up after overshooting the green. No one much notices my troubles.

I begin to see this as the essential lesson of Ireland: You are alone with your troubles. Later, when I tell this to the bartender at our hotel, he nods. "An Irish plays through all kind of shit. An Irish plays on."

One day, near Killarney, we run into some fair weather, a mere twenty-mile-an-hour wind, the sunshine glorious though intermittent. That day, we're off the links courses, away from the ocean, at the Killeen Course at Killarney Golf and Fishing Club. My caddie is a hard little guy named Bobby who doesn't want to hear that links golf is harder than the parkland version. "It's the same love grass," he tells me.

"Love grass?"

He points to the heather lining the secondary rough; it's nasty and innocent all at once, like the hair in your armpit. "The tall stuff," he says. "That's the love grass."

I'll bite. "Why do you call it love grass?"

He chomps down on his toothpick. "You go in there," he says, "and you're fucked for sure."

Today the sun shines. It has been five days of struggle, my best moments unwitnessed, my putting troubles tossed like dice around the dinner table. When I land in a trap at seventeen—the deepest trap, Bobby says, in all of Ireland—Bobby shakes his head.

"Tom," he says, "you have to tell yourself one thing."

I take the sand wedge from him and start up the fairway. "What's that?"

"There are always tougher shots than the one you have to hit," he says. "You have to convince yourself you are up to it."

I'm five days in. I have seen all manner of trouble. I am beginning to get golf muscles. The trap is probably twelve feet deep, with a sheer face, hugging the green. It takes the first Sullivan seven shots to get out, and even then he has to hit it out into the fairway to do it. My ball has slid back into a flat lie. My rounds used to collapse around moments such as this. I climb into the trap, place my weight on my left foot, open my club face absurdly far, and swing hard. The ball rises and settles fifteen feet from the pin. Simple. In a matter of moments, I will three-putt.

Bobby gives me a hand up out of the trap. One of the Sullivans murmurs something, but no one says much. It doesn't matter. It's just another tough shot. Bobby's right. There's a tougher shot somewhere in Ireland. I'm likely to see it tomorrow, or the next day, or on the next hole. I'm beginning to understand I'm up to it.

19 Crudup or Shut Up

IT'S RAINING ON THE FIRST TEE. POURING, ACTUALLY. For a second the whole thing staggers against the possibility of a rain-out. Billy Crudup locks eyes with me.

"Dude," he says, "I want to play. I'm a player." The rain, I tell him, doesn't scare me. "You're a player too, then," he says. He looks at the caddie. "We're players," he announces.

The caddie looks at us dubiously. Two nobodies on a Tuesday afternoon. In the rain. "I believe it," he says, acting as if he does.

We're playing Manhattan Woods, an ambitious new track across the Hudson River and fifteen miles up the Palisades Parkway from New York. Around the seventh hole the course lurches eastward, back in the direction of the skyline of the city, though the mist allows none of the view. John, the caddie, points to Crudup as he sets up for a shot. "He's got a nice, simple swing. What does he do for a living?" Like every caddie at every private course, this guy has carried bags for princes and kings, or at least he claims he has. Michael Jordan was here only a month ago, he tells me, with Ahmad Rashad. Crudup is an actor, I tell him "What's he been in?" the caddie asks.

"*Jesus' Son*," I say.

This makes him cringe. He looks at Crudup, who's showing his game now, his swing steady and low, his body completely still.

"That's a hell of a name for a movie," the caddie says. A moment later, he speaks again. "I'm thinking he had to have played the son. He's an awfully little guy."

Stars are big. Huge. Incomprehensibly large. So gigantic that the terms used to describe stars are conceptual: It would take five million Earths to fill this star. Things like that.

Billy Crudup, by contrast and by independent authority, is small. He insists that all his movie roles to date have been small, even his lead in *Waking the Dead,* though actually it was the movie that was small. "It was sort of one-weekish," he says.

He is extraordinarily talented and memorable, but only for very short time. In truth, thus far Billy Crudup has been a bit of a Zelig, a cipher, an invisible man. You probably have seen him in a film (he has made ten), enjoyed his performance very much, noted it, and then forgotten him entirely. And this, Crudup says, is the way he likes it. "I'm not a star," he says on the eleventh tee. "I have no desire to be one." That may be so—it really may be so. There is no greater challenge today than divining a man's heart and finding the truth when confronted with the none-of-this-is-important-to-me syndrome. It is a mental struggle, this search for truth. But one must try, or life loses meaning.

Instructive in this search is the knowledge that some popular entertainers would have you know that their purposes are more serious than entertainment, that their success at being creative is in itself a paradox, that they are more inward-focused and substantial than all that. Why do they do this? What could be more substantial than pleasing the masses? Than teaching us lessons through art? Than looking quite excellent, and having a smooth stroke, and setting a good example? This is a strange thing to contemplate.

Stranger still is that this same Billy Crudup is by acclamation in Hollywood the next thing, the actor who is scheduled to arrive this year, our next star. For example: "Billy is right there," says Walter Parkes, a producer of *Men in Black*. "He's as ready as you can be."

At the golf course, as in life, no one knows who he is. Earlier that morning, Crudup flopped his bag down, rattled his clubs, and shook hands with the caddie.

"I should have never agreed to play golf," Crudup said. "I can't keep my guard up if I'm trying to get into your head." Keep his guard up?

He ran his hands through his hair, which is long, thin, and fairly, well, dirty. "If you were my brother," he continued, "I'd be messing with you before we even set the stakes."

Warming up, Crudup drifted from one club to the next, going by the book, from a wedge to a seven-iron and on to the driver, hitting high, short drives that fell reliably and reasonably to the wet grass without a hint of a slice. I can't tell whether he's any good at all, but he certainly looks good. His game is creamy and soft, like butter. Slipping on his glove, he chats with the caddie. He blends in, using his sturdy set of Callaway clubs, his greasy hat, and his worn-out golf shirt as camouflage. Keep his guard up? Maybe this is acting. Maybe the guard is up and Billy Crudup is really working it. Maybe this is a full-out actor's representation of Tuesday morning.

Billy Crudup is an actor. A capital-A Actor, if you know what I mean. He played the marauding shooter in *Sleepers*, the creepy, charismatic Steve Prefontaine in *Without Limits*, the cruel older brother in *Inventing the Abbotts*, an unlucky rancher in the somnambulant *The Hi-Lo Country*. He was there. He was in them. You can rent them and check. In each film, he flashes across the screen, angry, angular, and is out of your way before you know it. Even if you remember him from such recent flameouts as *Waking the Dead* or *Jesus' Son*, odds are you never noticed him, not in the sense of connecting the dots between movies, between roles. "What distinguishes him is that he's not choosing parts to get the next part," says Bryan Lourd, an agent at CAA, which represents Crudup. "I always tell clients you have to be able to remember why you chose to do a movie, to always be able to look at a movie and know, whether it's good or bad, why you chose to do it. Billy does. He hasn't made one wrong move, either."

Who can say? Crudup hasn't really taken his shot. He's an unknown quantity in Hollywood, defined by supporting roles rather than by the spotlight, the guy who pulled himself out of consideration for Leo's role in *Titanic*. Whether this is taste or a lack of smarts seems to be a matter of interpretation for everyone except Crudup.

Let's talk about stars for a moment. A star is a spinning ball of fire. A star is a source of light and energy. A star shines. A star is the force that keeps the planets in orbit.

Billy Crudup is not a star. Billy Crudup doesn't want to be a star. He doesn't want any part of it. Not the hot gas nor the magnetic fields nor the responsibility of the various orbits of fame. He can't deal with the possibility of his own solar flares. Call him a star and he winces.

In the new Cameron Crowe movie, *Almost Famous*, the director's paean to rock 'n' roll in the '70s, the movie that many people expect will catapult Crudup toward fame whether he likes it or not, Billy Crudup plays a star.

"It's completely infectious," he says. "It's sick. We're at the Palladium, working with 1,700 extras. We walk out into the darkness. Then the roar, you know? When I come up on a solo, even though I'm working from playback and everybody knows it, I give them the little face—you know that little guitar face?—and they go fucking nuts. Berserk. You look into their eyes and they flip out." He's smiling now at the memory, at the whiff of power. "That is some pretty high-dosage shit. In an instant, you understand how people can get fucked up on that."

"It's a pretty narrow plank," Cameron Crowe says, "letting an actor play a rock star. And it's a pretty steep plunge when it doesn't work. There's very little crossover. It's hard to do convincingly. Billy succeeded because he cared so much. He had us believing.

"Led Zeppelin was referenced all through the movie, so we decided to show what we had to Robert Plant and Jimmy Page. We fly to London, and the two of them sit down to watch it, and I'm cringing. When it's over, Robert Plant gets up and starts pacing. He keeps saying, 'I know that guy.' And we say, 'Yeah, Billy Crudup! He's been in...' and Plant says, 'No, no, I know him, the guitarist. I've met that guy.' He was sure Billy was a pro." Crowe laughs. "That was a blinding moment. Billy had him. Robert fucking Plant."

Billy Crudup is not s star. Over and over again people walk right by him. Tell people who he is and they stare straight at him and squint. They get nothing on the radar. He looks like a kid. The hair. The ratty shirt. The shitty belt. He could be a waiter, a busboy, a farmer. He looks for all the world like someone you might meet three times a day. "The thing about Billy is that he takes two looks," says Crowe. "The first look: Fine. He's good-looking. All that. And the long look, that's where you see that he has all these levels. It's a subtle face."

Crudup actively and passively defies biography. He hates the mythology others (publicists, mostly) have set up for him—that he was a wrestler in college, that he's a master chess player—with only a marginal basis in fact. (He wrestled in high school. He watches chess in Washington Square Park.) Still, he displays the traditional movie star's refusal to help draw the picture, talking about himself only by discussing the roles he's played, forcing the conversations away from the facts of his life, even when people have them wrong.

For instance, he offers that he bought his car to share with his brothers, who also live in New York. It seems to me like a good, brotherly thing to do, a generous act, or at the very least somewhat thoughtful.

"Let me ask you about the car," I say.

"I wish you wouldn't," he says. "It's just a car." Crudup closes down. He's private about his family life, he says. But this is not family—this is a sport-utility vehicle. What's worse is that Crudup looks wounded that I would ask.

"You paint your picture of me, who I am, what I'm interested in, what I like, what I'm like when I'm not talking about a movie or whatever work I'm in." He's pensive now, squinting as he talks, reeling in the casual gestures, cooling the surface even more. "I do enough of these and people create this idea of what I am. Generally, this is something an actor works toward—avoiding certain subjects, promoting others, being seen in certain places, finding the right place to stand, being seen in certain causes. All of that is meant to promote a calculated image. That's work I'm not too interested in. If I start in on it, I have to maintain it." He holds his palms up and laughs. "The premise of all of this is that anybody would give a shit one way or the other, which I call into question almost immediately."

Even when he does talk about his roles (he refers to them as "choices," a term that implies calculation, pluses, and minuses), he insists that they are small, that they're not about him. Even his role in the Cameron Crowe movie, he says, is "small."

"Yeah," Crowe says, "so small that we end the movie on his face."

We're at the turn and Crudup is peeling an orange. The caddie eats a sandwich, waiting for us at the tenth hole. I ask about the Tom Stoppard play *Arcadia*, in which Crudup played a friend of Lord Byron's, his first big onstage role. It's an "actor's role," the kind of thing actors like to talk about. Crudup nods. "That was fun. I'm working with Tom Stoppard, being directed by Nunn—great fucking play. There's no way I can't take the job seriously, no way I can't see myself as the luckiest actor on the planet at that moment." But what's lucky? Are these the roles he wants more of? Or does he intend to move on, to press toward something else? Writing? Directing? "I don't write, and I don't want to. I want to act. I enjoy the work. I like being a tool, an implement for a great director. I got what I wanted here, on the stage."

At this point, I'm thinking: Be a star. Dazzle me, please. "I'll be expressive about that," he says, cranking his voice up a bit, for the first time showing a level of enthusiasm. But he sounds a little like your old man expressing the importance of maintaining an IRA. "I learn from the theater. The theater is more of an argument. I'd prefer an argument about movies, but no one ever brings one." Yeah, yeah. I try to think argument. Then I buy a sandwich.

There are many stars in the galaxy. Each star has a huge gravitational field. Stars send light out into space, where it travels many years, over distances we call light-years, until, sometimes, it reaches other stars. Stars exist in tension with one another. Billy Crudup lives with a star named Mary-Louise Parker, veteran stage and movie actress. She opens a play on the very day of our golf match. I wrangle a ticket, figuring it's a chance to talk to Crudup one more time, that maybe we'll get past the rhetoric and shake out something clearer.

It's funky going to the theater by yourself. Especially on opening night, when everybody is glittering and giddy. Maybe Crudup is right. Maybe you need to talk, to argue about a play before it means anything. I have a critic's seat, dead center, four rows up. Linda Lavin is sitting to my right. The whole thing feels a little lonely. The play is good, though, and Parker is just plain hot. She oscillates between being sexy and haggard, plays the character at different ages without a hitch, cranks around the stage in blue jeans, a housecoat, and a little black dress, all without once giving the sense that she is costumed. No one can take his eyes off her. In this pathetic way, I start to feel that I am not alone after all, that I'm in the presence of someone. I realize that I've been looking at her my whole life—in movies—and that she's made me feel who she is through movies, movies I didn't even really like—*Fried Green Tomatoes, Boys on the Side.* But she convinced me long ago. And she's convincing me tonight. The woman is a star.

Crudup is there, shaven, clothes crisp and unrumpled, looking impossibly younger (he's thirty-two) than he had on the golf course At intermission, he steps outside for a cigarette, where he talks feverishly to a young guy wearing the clunky black glasses that decorate the faces of New Yorkers now, lighting one cigarette off another, standing in the very spot where he picked me up in the family SUV that morning. Traffic rumbles by. The crowd is abuzz. No one locks in on Crudup, though he's looking for the first time today like a movie star—streetside, beneath the marquee, in the drizzle, Marlboro dangling from the corner of his mouth. He nods at several of them, stares a few people in the face. No one recognizes him. He seems to enjoy some power—being public, being open, being Crudup—that allows him to light himself slowly, throughout the day, until he illuminates into a look that tells people what he is, at least for the time being. The thing is, no one notices.

"It's a pretty good deal for me," he says of watching Parker work. "Because I don't have to go into it worried about what I'm going to say to her. She's not going to fuck up. She's just not going to fail. And

I know I can learn by watching her. That's why I go to the theater. So I'm just going to say thank you That's what most actors want."

I head back to the lobby to gawk at the still photos of Mary-Louise Parker. I'm thinking about her as I walk away from Crudup. It's fucked-up. I'm thinking that she's taller than I would have guessed, that she's bigger than he is. Still, I wouldn't guarantee it. It's an impression. She just feels bigger.

For a while, a rumor floated that Crudup might be cast in the next *Star Wars*. "That's a new one on me," he says. "Where do they get this shit?"

"What if it were true? Would you take it?"

"No chance," Crudup says without hesitation. "It's just not for me."

This is the essential Crudup assertion. Billy Crudup doesn't want it. Frankly, that's fine with me. I wouldn't want it, either But then again, I'm not an actor. One thing: Billy Crudup is an actor. He has an M.F.A. from NYU and stage credits from here to the end of your arm. Actor. Yes, sir. So I ask, directly, the one thing I've been wanting to ask: "Don't you want a big movie? Don't you want to take it up a notch, maybe just once? Wouldn't it be nice to have a generation remember you, talk about you, in that one really big picture? Gladiator. Good cop. Jedi knight Isn't that, at some level, the whole idea of the game?"

"Dude, that's what I am shooting for every time out. I want to crystallize like that in every performance. Just like that. Just like you were saying. Every fucking time."

He doesn't want it enough to care, but he cares just enough to want it. Another wonderful, slippery nugget, this mantra for slackers.

"When Billy makes it," says Cameron Crowe, "it'll be a kind of accident. People will say, 'Where did this guy come from?' And they'll go back and look at his record and they'll think they made this great discovery, when he's been there all along."

On the matter of stars: There are a lot of stars still being discovered. At the far edges of the galaxy, new stars are registered by astronomers all the time. These are marked as discoveries. These kinds of stars are often given numbers rather than names. If Crudup is a star, then maybe, just maybe, he's one of these stars at the very edge of our vision. ("He's a throwback to guys like Pacino and De Niro," Bryan Lourd says. "Like them, he's very smart, very understanding about the long haul. There's no rushing Billy. Because of that, he'll be around in thirty or forty years.") These stars are so far away that despite their size, despite their potential for energy release, they appear to us very tiny and insignificant. Their distance might make us mistake them for less than what they are.

If Crudup is going to become the next man, the real man, or the star, it will happen by accident, at the end of some period of hard work, at a time when no one expects him. People will recognize him without really knowing where they saw him. He wants this. He's not asking for much. To be forgotten, then remembered, then forgotten again.

At the end of the golf match, Crudup is defeated. We double the bet on the last hole and stand at the tee, looking up the hill toward the clubhouse. It's an enormous carry to the fairway. Crudup is taking practice swings, hoping for ten extra yards from his driver. He's standing askance again, looking away. From the side, I can see that he still could be anyone, a doper, a guitar player, someone famous. Or not. I wonder aloud if he's even old enough to remember Steve Prefontaine, the guy he played in *Without Limits*, the gnarly distance runner of the early seventies. So I ask. At this, the caddie perks up.

"You mean the runner?" he says.

"Yeah, Prefontaine."

"You're talking about the movie," he says.

"Absolutely."

"I saw that. *Without Limits*. I just rented that. Now, that was a movie. A good movie."

"Billy was in it," I say.

The caddie looks puzzled, shakes his head. "No, the guy's name was Steve."

"No, I'm talking about Billy," I say. Crudup grins.

"Who?"

"Him. He was in the movie."

"The guy was a runner."

"That's what I'm saying," I say. "He played the runner."

"That guy was a lot bigger." The caddie pauses, and then it clicks. "That was you? Yeah, it was. Oh, man, I saw that. I just saw that. Now, that was a movie. That was you?"

Crudup is smiling.

(20) Long Drivers

YOU GOTTA FIGURE EVEN MONKEYS CAN PUTT. Give ten thousand monkeys ten thousand putters and at least one of them is going to nail a ninety-foot snake through a double-break before too long. But hand them a forty-nine-inch, oversized titanium driver with a stiff graphite shaft, and not a one will crank the ball 350 yards into the slot. Not in ten thousand years. Forget opposable thumbs! Being long-off-the-tee makes us human.

Everybody wants to be long. Hit it straight, sure. Gussy up your grip. Lean on your short game. Enjoy! But smack a long hard draw to the far end of a narrow landing zone and you're at the heart of it. You're there. You're long. In golf, as in the locker room, length is pretty self-evident. The long hitter leaves it out there, while the short hitters wrap themselves in cheap towels.

Any golfer who says they don't care about being long-off-the-tee is a damned liar. In most circles "long" means hitting the balls three hundred yards consistently. But when a mid-handicapper really throws himself at one from the white tees, he's likely sending the ball a little more than two hundred yards, then rolling another twenty or thirty. In the fairway, he checks a sprinkler head, walks off a few steps, subtracts the distance to the green, splits some differences, and pencils himself in at three hundred yards off the tee. But for most golfers, hitting it three hundred yards on a flat surface is a fantasy. For some, doing it even once is an impossibility.

The first step in getting long-off-the-tee is to figure out how short you really are. Striding boldly to the range tees with the primal weapon, the driver, in one hand and a surveyor's wheel in the other, I took some measurements at the range, sure that I could top three hundred. Loading and reloading, wheeling and re-wheeling the distance, the best I could manage was 272 yards, mostly roll, off a wonderfully high first bounce.

Stymied, I focused on three elements: equipment, technique and competition. My driver, I decided, sucked. It was killing me, robbing me of natural yardage. My swing, which allows me my marginal handicap, had to go. Finally, I had to see the long ball in person, to get a sense of the possibilities.

So I called Art Sellinger, the dean of the long drive, two-time national long- drive champ, for whom length is a craft, a piece of the game to be developed and nurtured. He was optimistic about my quest. "I feel good about this," he said. "I know we can add thirty to forty yards to your drive. I just know it." I liked his projection. Thirty more yards would take me over three hundred yards, I told him. Hearing that, he paused. "Well, then we can work on getting you some real distance," he said, inviting me to the RE/MAX North

American Long Drive Championship, the U.S. Open of long driving, where the forty-eight longest hitters in the country were waiting to humble me.

These are professional long-ball men. While they can all play
tee-to-green, they make their scratch hammering the ball at exhibi-
tions, corporate outings, and on one of the two long-ball tours. The
longest among them include Sean "The Beast" Fister, a former SEC
pole vaulter, who drove a 345-yard par four the first day he ever
played the game at twenty-four, winning the championship eight
years later; current two-time champ Jason Zuback, a Canadian
pharmacist and power-lifter, who plays the event with fourteen different drivers jammed in his bag; and '93 champ Brian Pavlett, a former Division 1 pitcher, whose classic swing and good looks seem
perfect for the part of a golf-pro. When I ask him about this, he bristles. "I'm not a golf pro. I'm a long driver."

How long are they? "Only rookies ask about numbers," Fister
drawls, reaching into his bag for yet another driver, one of the thirty prototypes he'll bring to the competition, tossing each aside as he
caves the face after twenty to thirty swings. But numbers can be had.
Fister once hit a 404-yard carry over a Canadian river for a radio
station gimmick. Zubak won the championship the year before by
driving a ball into a slightly uphill grid, forty yards across. The ball
came to rest at 351 yards. Fister snorts when I bring this up. "It ain't
about numbers. Long driving is all about the moment. You and the
ball. I might be able to hit one five hundred yards under the right
conditions. They just don't know." The "they" he refers to must surely be the covey of club-makers who congregate at the edge of the
driving range, watching the long drivers press their equipment to

maximum human tolerances. These guys represent the outside of the human envelope.

The first key to figuring the long drivers is easy. They swing fast. Faster than anyone you know. Faster than PGA pros. Zuback's club speed regularly measures 155 miles per hour; Fister has reached 170. The average PGA pro generates 126. This comforted me until I convinced the Taylor Made people to clock my swing— eighty-two miles per hour. Figuring I just wasn't swinging hard enough, I whirled on the ball as hard as I could. Ninety-four mph. The ball screamed low and left, duck-hooking inside the hundred-yard marker 150 yards to my left. Where do the pros get this club speed? Almost all of them are extraordinarily limber, allowing for a far greater hip turn. All of them have the thick agile frames of Division I athletes and the strength to match.

Does their equipment give them an edge? After all, they use the best drivers available, with cutting-edge shafts. In what seemed to me the ultimate shortcut to a longer drive, Sellinger upgraded my driver to a forty-eight-inch Ti Bubble 2, the Sellinger Special, which made my forty-four-inch driver feel like kindling. The angle and perspective from the top of a club this long is akin to the sensation of sitting in a Porsche for the first time. It smells good and seems fast even when its not moving, but you're not sure you can drive it, as everything is so different from your shitty Honda that you're not even sure where to put your hands.

Sellinger takes some time to get me set. "With a long club, the tendency is to want to swing slow," he says. "Forget that. Think smooth. To generate the speed, you have to work hard on your turn, take the club way back, then fire through with the hips." He inches me into a wider stance and urges me to line up off the front of my left foot rather than the heel. "You have to hit the ball coming up. That's where the longer club will help you." The ball shoots a little higher as I learn to trust my hands. "You have to round out your swing, while bringing your hands through hard. It's like a baseball swing, except on a different plane, but every corporate golfer I've seen blames their bad swing on their baseball swing. I always wonder if they ever hit a baseball cutting across the ball like that."

The club is scary; the swing feels awkward, but as with all good things in golf, I can sense the changes working. I'm hitting it square, trying hard not to read the yardage. Sellinger declares me ready to hit a few in a group with the big boys. I convince them to hit into the markerless expanse of the desert, from a bluff even, the idea being that I might find a little extra distance in the roll, that I wouldn't feel so absolutely naked with my hinky little fade, hitting from on high. I give them all Balatas, the softer, higher-spin ball, presumed by most to be shorter, while I load up with a hundred compression surlyn-covered pellets. We take aim at a distant pair of trees, my target of choice, as they seem out of reach, impossibly long. I estimate them at five hundred yards. Pavlett hammers his first ball thirty feet over them on the fly. Zuback hits a ball that crests as it passes over them.

"Geez," I say. "How far out are they?"

Sellinger shrugs. "Not too far. Three-thirty, maybe."

The time comes for me to take off my towel and take a shot. The big boys urge me on. Widen up. Stay strong. Keep your spine straight. I hit my first ball thin, but straight, and only Zuback comments, "Right down the middle."

"Screw you," I think as I reload. On the next one, the takeaway feels smooth, so I gear down; as my hands come through, I feel a good release, and the ball launches towards the trees. It won't get there, I can tell, but it might roll there. The big boys are all smiles, high-fiving me before it lands. I can't see where it settles, if it even makes the trees. What does it matter? I figure length is relative.

21 Golf in the Kingdom

IN GOLF, AS IN DANCE CLUBS, IT'S ALL ABOUT THE ropes—pressing up against the ropes, getting past the ropes, playing behind the ropes. At a tournament, the crowd bellies up to the cord, and there is Gary Player or Greg Norman or Fred Couples, solitary and isolated by green space. He's close, not twenty feet from the nearest spectator, but he couldn't be any farther away.

He's inside the ropes.

Enter the pro-am, the breed of tournament designed to give average players the chance to play alongside the pros. Amateurs pay to enter. Big. A typical pro-am runs a day and a half before a PGA Tour event and is populated by midrange touring pros teamed with local weathermen, CFOs, and your average barnyard collection of salesmen of the year.

And then there is the Hassan II Golf Trophy, the world's most exclusive pro-am, which features first-class jet service to Morocco, eight days of golf on four good tracks, black-tie dinners, a luncheon with the king, a night at the palace, drivers and hostesses at your command, and a friendly contingent of top-rank pros such as Player, Billy Casper, Seve Ballesteros, and Colin Montgomerie.

Whereas the average pro-am is about getting inside the ropes, if only for an afternoon, the Hassan II Trophy, named for the late king of Morocco, is about *living* inside the ropes—for eight days, anyway.

My caddie is a tall guy with a cad's mustache. He introduces himself as Mustafa and thrusts my bag onto his shoulder like it is an after-thought. On the practice tee, he watches me the way a bigger, stronger teenager eyeballs a rich kid. There seems to be the urge on his part to fight me because, as he says, I don't finish. He repeats it again and again. The seventh time he says it, I mutter to myself, "Bite me."

"I not bite you," he says. "I'm to take care of you. Finish the swing."

Four holes in, I have scalded a one-iron into a patch of cork trees, which line the course. Mustafa picks up three nuts from the ground and cracks one with his teeth.

"*Qu'est-ce que c'est?*" I ask.

"*Le balote*," he says. He makes a fist and punches himself in the gut. "Good for you."

The next day, as I'm standing over a long downhill putt, Mustafa says, "Be a man. Finish the putt." Then he hands me a nut, peeled and ready to eat. There is the same fist gesture, clenched at the waistline.

My partner today, the great Mexican pro Rafael Alarcon, laughs. "Those nuts will make you perform." I give him a look. "They're like that pill. They make you hard."

I laugh and eat the nut.

The next day, I'm playing alongside Johanna Head, a Brit from the Ladies European Tour. Mustafa gives me the same fist, the same little smile, and the peeled nut just before he hands me the driver. Amazingly, I'm starting to finish my swing, just as he'd ordered. I bite the nut. "Those are hallucinogenic, I'm afraid," Johanna says. Mustafa can't understand her. He looks from me to her, makes the fist, takes a step back. "You need to eat about eight," Jonanna says. "You'll hallucinate."

"Eight?" I say.

"Yes," Mustafa says suddenly. "Hit?"

"No," I say. "Eight."

"Yes. Hit."

And that's how it runs in Morocco. A number becomes a word. One story becomes another story. You rip your shots toward the horizon with purpose in front of small galleries of confused Moroccans who think you might be someone worth watching. Once in a while, you even get a round of applause. You are—despite your hinky fade, your lack of cubes around the greens, and your bagful of mismatched logo balls—inside the ropes.

Billy Casper is a big guy, bigger now than ever. It was Casper who, along with his good friend the late Hassan II, created this pro-am. The lumbering Mormon flat-stick expert and the diminutive Islamic monarch: a bizarre team if there ever was one.

Casper is giving an 8:00 A.M. putting lesson to a gynecologist from Los Angeles behind the dieseling bus in the parking lot of the Rabat Hilton. Amal, the doorman, looks at him. "Billy Casper," he says. "This is the greatest putter of all the times."

"Do you play golf?" I ask. He's a skinny little guy, maybe twenty-three, but he's tall and he can really toss the luggage.

"It's too much. I am with basketball. Do you know coaches?" I shake my head. Casper's wife whisks through the doors. Amal lifts an eyebrow. "She is maybe not a good putter."

"How do you know that?" I say.

"Women," he says. "Maybe they can't putt."

This is the way with these guys; they qualify and mitigate every assertion with "maybe" and "perhaps." When I tell this to Mustafa, he smiles. "You are learning. Morocco is a land of uncertainty."

I have been stalking Gary Player since I got here, and my encounter comes late on the sixth day. By this point, I have played 189 holes of golf. I've played my hands raw. The tips of my fingers are numb. My eyes are set in a permanent squint. I've taken a putting lesson from Billy Casper and hit balls with Seve Ballesteros, but I meet Player when he joins my foursome for a hotel shuttle ride.

Gary Player is oddly regal, clinging to a pair of golf shoes in the front seat. He travels a lot, he says. I ask him what it's taught him. He boils it down to a single lesson: "I have trouble with white bread," he says.

His eyes snap this way, then that, looking for a reaction. "Really," he says. "Americans have all the best food. Oranges. My God! You have miraculous oranges! What I'm saying is that white bread is the American cross to bear. It makes a big lump in your stomach. Have you ever stuck a piece of bread in a bowl of milk? It just forms a lump! A lump, I tell you!"

"So you don't like white bread," I say, rolling my eyes.

"Right," he says. "I never touch it! And you shouldn't, either. There's a message for America! Take that back to the children! Just give up the white bread! Please!"

From the back, someone says, "All bread?"

He puts his hands out in front of him like a nervous salesman fearing the kibosh, calming things, the pooch about to be screwed. "No, no. I'm talking about white bread only. Bleached flour. It didn't even exist a hundred years ago. Your system's not ready for it."

At this point, I can't resist. "What about rye bread?"

Player sounds a little panicky. We're missing his point. "I have no problem with rye bread. It's that soft white bread. It just kills me to see young people eating it. Kills me, I tell you."

Another voice from the back: "What about banana bread?"

On one of the last afternoons, I come across Billy Casper, sitting in a lawn chair, mopping his forehead, only slightly unhappy with shooting an eighty-eight. He asks if I'm having a good time.

I'm a little hungover and craving a hamburger, but I tell him I am. I ask how he's feeling. "I'm missing the king," he says. "He was a friend. It's all a little strange without him." The wind blows in from the sea, along the passages made by the cork trees. "I love this country," Casper says. "I've always wanted people to discover it. The king wanted that, too. We were in it together."

Casper looks at me then. "Do you miss your family?"

"Sure," I say. "But I'll be home in a day or two."

Casper stands. "See, that's just it," he says. "I think this is my home. In some ways. Part of my family is missing."

In the lobby, there are thirty-five photos of the late king play-ing golf on Dar Es-Salam, the home course he had Robert Trent Jones Sr. build for him in 1971. He was a stern, muscular little man. He looks to the distance in each photograph, as if tracking a shot or regarding a monument. Despite the great golfers who have played and won the tournament here—Casper, Payne Stewart—no golfers besides the king are pictured.

It seems pretty powerful and pretty stupid at the same time. Still, looking at him here, I get the sense that he was like everyone else who has come here to play. There he was, inside the ropes, alone with his game, intent on banging the next shot a little closer, or a lit-tle farther. Like any golfer, he probably liked someone to say, "Nice shot!" before they picked up and moved on.

(22) John Daly, Happy at Last

JOHN DALY GREETS ME IN HIS THURSDAY-morning uniform—XXXL Razorbacks T-shirt, beltless blue jeans, and tube socks. He might have rolled out of bed in these very clothes. He runs a hand over his stubble; a goatee appears to be rising. His head has been clipped to a uniform length. His eyes are crusty, narrowing in the sunlight. He would appear to be a mess.

"Long night?" I ask.

"Yeah, we had some boys over," he says. "Playing a little three-card poker, drinking a bunch of beer. Made one helluva mess." He slips on a pair of shades—the trademark Oakleys, which sit on his face all yellow and loose, giving him a remarkable distance, even at close range. His eyes relax behind the glasses. He is smiling.

He's not big. At least, not like I expected. Maybe five-eleven, maybe 225. He has gained weight since he started drinking again last year, just as he gained it when he quit drinking several years ago, just as he gained it when he started drinking again before that. He drops the weight; then he gains it back. It's just part of the ride. He doesn't care.

He's remodeling a house in Dardanelle, Arkansas, at the foot of the Ozarks, and, like him, the house is deep in process. A gate but no fence. An expanse of mud lying in wait for heavy rolls of sod. A slab of concrete. The outline of a pool sprayed on the ground in red paint. The only finished element appears to be the driveway, which is dotted with brass medallions, each stamped with the logo of his beloved Razorbacks of the University of Arkansas. "I'm tearing all this out," Daly says, waving an arm at the driveway. "It doesn't show off the Hogs the way I want." He scratches his chin again, the feathering of whiskers. He's thinking, reminding himself of something, checking something off a mental list. "I gotta call that guy," he says. Then he looks at me as if I might be that guy himself. "I gotta call him today." On the mountainside above him, past the golf course behind him, a gunshot rings out.

If there was a party here last night, if people were drinking and smoking cigarettes and spilling beer, there is no sign of it now. The kitchen is as clean as it can be, sunlight pouring in a column to the sink. The walls of each room are plastered with the memorabilia of celebrity, tracing the tortured path that John Daly has walked since 1991, the year of his improbable win at the PGA Championship, a tournament played that year on a particularly nasty, notoriously long course called Crooked Stick. He entered as an alternate, a twenty-five-year-old unknown, and won the thing without playing a practice round. It was a fine moment for golf. The good ol' boy rises on a jet trail of luck, raw power, and determination to claim the title, to trade shots with the best in the world. He gave hope to all golfers, even the outsiders, dispelling the image of the sport as a distraction of the rich. With the lumpy haircut, the beer gut, and the clothes he had paid for himself, Daly represented anything but the golf we'd come to know. And when he held the trophy over his head, he either swaggered or swayed. From the start, it was tough to say.

A reproduction of the $320,000 check he won at Crooked Stick hangs now above a lowboy in his dining room, as do various framed newspaper clippings trumpeting everybody's favorite John Daly stories—victory and sobriety—recording the scandals in tone, if not fact:

Daly emerges from Betty Ford with new focus.

Daly stuns the world again at St. Andrews.

Daly threatens wife, court date set.

Daly's divorce final.

Alone again, Daly quietly finds focus.

Daly drinking again.

Wilson signs Daly.

Daly trashes hotel room.

Wilson drops Daly.

Daly sober again.

Callaway signs Daly.

Callaway covers Daly's $1.7 million gambling losses.

Callaway drops Daly.

Daly drinking again.

As I scan the wall, Daly looks over my shoulder, taking it all in.

"There's a lot there," he says. "Don't you think?" There's not one bit of it he won't talk about, either. He will win again, he says, this year or next. And as for sobriety, well, the hell with it. "I got tired of showing myself as something I wasn't," he says before we even sit down, leaning against an island in his kitchen, wiping the counter with a sponge in ordered, precise swipes. "Sometimes I would quit on my own, and that was fine. But when I wanted a drink, I wanted a drink. Just like anybody else. It wasn't like I wanted a drink or I would die."

Anyone familiar with the rehab ethos knows how we're supposed to deal with this sentiment. Denial is a cruel master, they'll say. Yea, though he walk through the valley of rationalization. . . . I remind him that the Twelve-Steppers expect this. He shakes his head.

"The worst mistake I ever made was admitting that I was an alcoholic," he says, "because I gave them all the power. According to them, there's only one way to go. Now, I either go that way or everybody writes me off."

With that, he lights another cigarette. "Man, I am hungry."

The phone rings and Daly leaves me there, standing among the stories and photos. One thing this wall of clippings shows is that, over the past decade, he has been unable to reconcile the various versions of himself. In one moment he is John Glenn, straight out of the heartland, improbably orbiting the massive, insular professional game, giving everyone a look at it from the jarring perspective of outer space. And in the next he is Gus Grissom, blowing the door too quickly, losing the capsule, drowning in flames.

I'm looking at a stock photo of Daly, deep in his backswing, knee cocked, club fully past parallel. It is a sight—Daly all coiled up, preparing to lash. It is a swing with its own motto, a swing worth seeing in person. Truth be told, if you could see only four things on the PGA Tour, you'd want to see Augusta, follow Tiger for a round, catch Arnold Palmer before he's gone, and watch John Daly hit balls at the practice range.

When Daly hits the range, it is a bit like an eclipse. People seem to be afraid to look directly at him, at it—the John Daly event. They judge him, they mutter about wasted talent, as if he owed them the act of tying the loose ends, as if they had a stake in his career. They trade stories, nod like sages, as he works his way from one club to the next, smoothly corkscrewing himself through to his high, limber finish. John Daly is the longest hitter in the game. Says so right here in these headlines: Long John Daly. He's also got one of the best short games in the world, but he struggles with the putter. He laughs when he plays. Really laughs. He's also everybody's favorite train wreck.

When Daly finally reenters the kitchen, he's got a cell phone in the crook of his neck. He's on hold with his sod supplier, and before this whole interview thing starts, he wants to emphasize that he knows what he's learned. He wants to get that out of the way. "I'll tell you my lessons," he says, tagging his fingers one by one. "I don't drink and drive. I don't drink every day. I don't drink to get drunk." He grabs a Diet Coke from a cooler on the kitchen floor and jingles his keys in his pocket. "It's all common sense. You can figure that out on your own. I read the *Twelve Steps*. I know the book. I respect the steps. I think about them every day.

He looks out the window. He's done for now. John Daly wants to eat.

We're on the streets of Dardanelle in Daly's black Mercedes. Riding shotgun is his twenty-three-year-old girlfriend, Shanae, a former Big 12 Conference hurdler who gazes out the window disinterestedly. She's got a bootleg Milli Vanilli CD playing just for laughs. "I'm just wearing this out," she says. "It's hard to find. It's not legal." She has a tired look about her. She wants to go work out, but instead she's here with us, going for fast food at 10:45 in the morning. In the back, next to me, is Daly's friend Bud Still, a Buy.com Tour player currently crashing at Daly's house. He's struggled with his game lately, having botched the Q-School last November, and he's come to hang with Daly in preparation for the next few months of Monday qualifiers. He has an Arkansas hat pushed back on his head, his forehead bracketed by the requisite Oakleys. They crack each other up.

"Two choices," Daly says. "Taco Bell or McDonald's."

"Ain't no choice!" Bud shouts. "Ain't no choice at all! I need a burger. I need a burger bad."

Daly snorts. The road thumps by. Barbecue shacks. Muffler shops. Video stores. Dalyscape. He loves it here. He points to a mountain in the distance. "That's our famous Mount Nebo," he says.

Shanae perks up. "That's where John proposed to me."

"What's up there?" I ask.

"I don't know," Daly says. "Fish fries. I believe they have a lot of fish fries up there." No one comments. A dog runs alongside the car, then quits.

At the drive-through, Daly orders by numbers. "Ones and fours for everybody." He supersizes all of us without asking. Was there any question?

The kid at the window doesn't seem to recognize him or even notice the gleaming car. When I offer to pay, Daly shakes his head. "You're in my town now. I'll take care of you."

"That's right," Bud says. "This is John's town. Every bit of it. Just look at it." That just cracks them up.

Daly eats methodically, and his burger seems to vanish, bite by bite, in the moments I look away. He's rambling a little, discussing his most recent trip to rehab, made at the insistence of Ely Callaway, Daly's sponsor at the time. He lasted less than a day. "People say I turned around at the gate. That ain't right. I went in. I was there overnight. The place was filthy. Right away, patients were telling me they could get me booze, reefer, cocaine. I figured, screw it. I knew what was going on."

The moment he checked himself out of rehab, Daly said goodbye to a reported three-million-dollar endorsement deal, parting with his second sponsor in three years. Six months later, he remains the only proven draw on the PGA Tour, or in any sport for that matter, without a huge compensation package from a major corporate sponsor.

Daly shifts in his seat, sucks on his Diet Coke, and casts an eye at the corners of the room. "They took away every choice, even the little ones. It just wore me down. Really, the hardest part for me was they wouldn't let me have Diet Coke. Cigarettes, yes. Cokes, no. It made no sense. At Betty Ford, at least they tried to teach you. This place was the opposite. They said they had their reasons. But I had just had it. People think I walked out because I couldn't handle it. I just didn't respect the method. Not there, anyway." He lights a cigarette, draws on it as if climbing a rope. He glances back at a corner. "Cobwebs," he mutters.

Daly is a gentle guy. Today, anyway. He moves tentatively, as if he might upset the entire room with a single turn. He's heavy and hard to stir, and the way he fusses and tidies up around the house is less than intimidating. He doesn't mind throwing stuff all over the table—cups, ashtrays, receipts, letters, napkins—but when he stands to leave the room, he cleans up. "I hate a mess," he says.

Shanae shakes her head. "He's a neatnik. Drives me crazy."

Daly wipes the table, then stands at the sink, rinsing. "I tried all those drugs. I took Paxil and Prozac; they made me feel like a ghost. I didn't want to play. I didn't care enough to practice. I don't care for those drugs. I don't see any answer there.

"You can be addicted to meat, as far as I'm concerned," he says, looking me in the eye and laughing. "Why else would I eat six cheeseburgers a day?' When I point out that he might be blurring the line between addiction and compulsion, he agrees. "Then there's a whole lot of compulsion in the world." He pauses. "Dammit! I gotta call Rico!" He excuses himself and disappears into the bedroom for another call. He darts away for these calls so often, I begin to wonder if he's doing it for punctuation.

At five o'clock, John Daly has a light beer. The alcoholic's big moment. Okay, I say to myself, here we go: This is when he'll roll off the cliff. He cracks the can without a flourish, without the standard late-afternoon paean to the day's first beer. An hour ago, Bud poured me an absurdly large Crown and Coke, and I've been slurping wolfishly at my plastic cup ever since. I'm buzzed. "I'll tell you what," Daly says eventually. "You boys are going to need some more whiskey."

He holds up the bottle and measures: Three fingers left. He might as well be looking at a rock or a hammer, a brick. No hunger. Bud has told me Daly doesn't drink whiskey. I shrug. "Want me to get some?"

"Nah," Daly says. "Too far. You shouldn't drive."

Daly sniffs the air, hits on the beer, then digs around in a big jar of Life Savers, roots out a cherry one, and pops it in his mouth. He snaps his fingers in mock inspiration. "We need to play some music. Do you play?" he asks me, strumming an air guitar.

I know two chords, which I learned one night on a bender and have remembered ever since. "Only if I'm drunk enough," I say.

Daly laughs, rolling the Life Saver in his mouth. "Do what you can, then," he says. "'Cause I want to play."

Shanae, however, doesn't want to play. She wants to talk. To John. She's back in the kitchen, clamoring for his attention. It reminds me of a family scene, the kind of moment, littered with contrary tensions and desires, that I play out in the shiny kitchens of my brothers- and sisters-in-law. Every once in a while, Shanae pulls open her robe to flash John. "Do you like this muscle, baby?" she says, flexing her thigh.

Bud averts his eyes. "Oh, Lord," he says. "Don't go there."

I'm filming it all with a digital camera, which I'm using instead of a tape recorder for the interview. Daly loves it. "That's a helluva thing," he says of the camera, taking his eyes off Shanae. "You know, I have a couple of those."

"A couple?"

"They give them away at different tournaments." He takes the camera from my hand, regards it the way you might regard a geode.

"I didn't even know what they were." He walks out and comes back in after a minute, cradling two cameras and their attachments. Pretty soon, we're all filming one another—me filming Daly, Daly filming Shanae, Bud filming all of it—and witness to what, exactly? Four people, a kitchen, a bag of chips. Shanae still wants John's attention. She pulls back her robe. "Don't show me that, baby!" he says, filming away. "Not unless you want to put on a show." Bud starts fixing the two of us each another Crown and Coke. We decide to move to Seagram's next, since we're out of Crown. Daly nurses his beer. He wants to play a game.

"If I was an animal," he says to me, "what animal would I be?"

This is an old interview trick, a stupid one, the kind of ice-breaker Regis Philbin would ask, only Daly's got it all turned. He's asking *me* about *him*. But I'm drunk, so I fuzz up my eyes and take a long look.

"A bear, maybe," I say.

He shakes his head. "That's taken."

"You could be an alligator." I like that.

"Nah, man, they're ugly. I ain't a gator."

"You could be a lion," I say. And it could work, too—the hair, shaved close to the head now, that will be golden by summer; the low-slung bulk; the whiskers; the huge, broad face, friendly and sad all at once.

Daly's pleased. "You got it! Chi Chi Rodriguez called me that once. He said, 'You're like a lion, scaring everybody, stalking around.' I try to think of myself as a lion, bringing down the kill, controlling the jungle. A lion controls his jungle." He nods. "I control the jungle. That's the way I see my days now."

Bud echoes an amen, cracking another Diet Coke to mix with the whiskey.

An hour later, Daly says something about playing cards and I perk up. "I hate to take your money, Tom," he says.

Bud cackles. "You'll be giving it to him, Tom. He's good."

"I am not," Daly says. "I lost ninety bucks last night. That was hard enough. I just don't enjoy poker that much."

With Daly, issues of money are totally skewed. Eating 1.7 million at the casinos seems to have hurt him less than the ninety dollars he dropped in Dardanelle last night. But, as usual, he is utterly at ease with his habits and launches into the saga of his gambling, not as a cautionary tale so much as a casino travelogue. He says he started with blackjack, then Caribbean stud, then craps, before finally settling in at the slots, eventually working his way from the one-hundred-dollar to the five-hundred-dollar machines.

"Slots are great. You work them for hours, look up, and people are watching you; you look back down and you'd never know they were there. The slot machines are like being completely alone, on my own, like on a cross-country drive. When you check your watch, thirty hours have gone by. It was scary how far away I got." There came a time when he was routinely taking $500,000 markers to keep it rolling, and it's estimated that he blew ten million over a three-year period. "I can't do that again. I just can't. I have to be like everybody else. Drink the free drinks. Play with my stake. No credit cards. No markers."

Shanae rubs the back of his head. Bud changes the CD. Daly looks at me, squinting. "You need anything?" he says. He's suggesting a Coke, an iced tea, something to eat. "You need anything at all?" Five minutes pass, and then he has forgotten I'm there. It's like that with Daly. He seems to care too much one moment and then not in the least the next. That may explain why he's been able to hold on to so many friends in the mercurial world of the PGA Tour, where spirits rise and fall with each coming Thursday. He bears no grudges and knows better than to run down fellow players. "Everybody is somebody's best friend" is his refrain. At one point, though, he is microwaving cheese dip, sighing deeply at the name of David Duval, who Daly says backed out of playing with him at a team event last fall. "It was just disappointing. My game was coming around. I was starting to really hit it. David backs out, and next thing I know he's there with Freddie Couples."

"Freddie!" Bud says.

Daly looks up, raises an eyebrow. "Can't really blame him, can you?" That cracks them up again.

It's eight-thirty. Bud and I are drunk. He's pounding me on the shoulder. "John has done so much for me," he says. "Nobody knows. People say there's a king. . . ." He weaves up the stairs.

I'm thinking Elvis, and then, surprisingly, I say it out loud.

"Man, fuck Elvis!" Bud says, laughing. "I'm talking about Arnold Palmer. He was the king! But now, that's what I'm telling you: John is the king. John Daly is the king!"

"Tell me a story," I say.

"He helps me out. He's helped me out all along. Money. Friendship. I feel like it's a blood thing. John'll let me stay with him for as long as I need. He'll drive me anywhere. Give me the shirt off his back. You know, friendship. He didn't have to reach out to me. I'm no one. We're both crazy about the Razorbacks, but aside from that, I'm no one."

Daly won't hear of that. "Buddha," he says. "You are not no one."

Bud shrugs. "I know I ain't no one."

Daly laughs. "Shit, Buddha, I'm not saying that. I'm saying you are somebody. Not that you ain't nobody."

"I got you," Bud says.

When I sit down on the couch, Bud gives me the once-over.

"Man, those glasses suck." He reaches into my shirt pocket, pulls out my sunglasses, and, before I can say a word, snaps them in half. "You need Oakleys!" He takes the glasses off his head and hands them to me. Daly watches from the couch, laughing. He wants to watch *South Park*, but he'll wait, because Bud is so excited he's shouting. "Now, those are glasses! Isn't that right, John? This boy needs Oakleys! Damned right." He seems to feel I have been pulled into a brotherhood by slipping on his glasses.

Daly laughs, reaches into his pocket, and holds out his own Oakleys. "Here, take these, too, Tom. Then you get two for one."

Being with John Daly on a night like this—in a room crammed with the twenty guitars, the eighty-two signed jerseys, the small studio, and the snaking sectional leather couch—sipping that sickening mixture of Coke and whiskey, one senses the absolutely familiar amid the foreign. Voices rise. Bud hoots. The arguments are routine. The Cotton Bowl. New York City. Sailing versus skiing. We take our sides, inevitably, and argue from the holster of our regional prejudices. I love the Mets. Daly is a Braves fan, so I prod him about John Rocker. "I know the Braves love him," he says. "He can really throw it." He won't say anything either way about Rocker's racist comments. "I can't get on him for a mistake. They'd better not suspend him, not for something he said."

"People forget," I say, "that you have a right to be an asshole." Daly rolls it around in his head for a second. "And every asshole is somebody's best friend."

After an hour, Bud pours more whiskey. "You go, girl," Daly says to Bud, sliding himself down into the recesses of the couch. Shanae throws a leg over him. He slaps her on the thigh. "Come on," he says, "I need you to sing." Shanae is tired.

Daly rides in a gear somewhat lower than most. He untwists a story, begs Shanae to sing, restlessly clears the table with the same low energy that drives like a bass line beneath the chaos. "I can't stand a mess," he says, arm crooked around the bottle of Crown, brimming ashtray in his palm. Whereas he drank the first beer slowly, he wolfs the next one in an instant, thoughtlessly and without passion. He stands, powering up his amps, testing the mics. He's focusing on the night, on the music, on setting up the moment.

I'm looking hard at Daly, trying to figure out what this drinking is all about. I see no desperation, no real anxiety, none of the fearful hunger of the inveterate boozer. In the parlance, I suppose he'd be called a binge drinker. All told, he's had six, maybe seven beers. We've lived the day like frat boys, shooting the shit, eating McDonald's for lunch, diving into a bowl of cheese dip for dinner, pop-snapping Diet Coke after Diet Coke. There is no transformation with the first beer, or even through the next five. He does not up the ante. He does not want to drive. He does not switch to hard liquor. He doesn't show any flashes of anger. He looks like the same guy who greeted me this morning. I could easily be spending time with my brother, running down the same subjects—college football, lost nights, women we knew, the shape of the beer gut. The fuel for the night is not booze; it's conversation. It's a comforting life here, rife with reinforcement, admiration, and love. Family life.

At six-fifteen, I wake in a high queen-sized bed, wedged in a gathering of pillows. Joe Montana's jersey leers from the wall above, pressed and signed but still ready to play. I stumble downstairs for a pee.

Someone has cleaned the house. By now I can be sure it was John, sneaking up early to clear the decks so that the sun might creep in along the proper lines. Standing in his dining room, I read a few of the framed stories, the ones he's chosen to remember. On the wall, there are pictures of his daughters, Shynah and Sierra. Him holding them up; them wrapping their arms around one another. They reach for him in each shot, sticky or sandy or covered in cake.

Each photo of Daly presents a version of the man so entirely different from the last that standing here is like looking at pictures of seven brothers, seven silly men, each of them similar to the one before, each entirely defined by a given trait. Daly trips along the years, sleepy or grumpy, bashful or dopey. A clock ticks loudly from his desktop, a surface littered with crystal paperweights, stacked high with the documents of his life—contracts and letters. Promises and pleas stand at the ready. The crack of dawn in Dardanelle. My head throbs. The sun sets up its scrim in the morning windows.

Upstairs again, I prop myself up in the bed and snap on *SportsCenter*, vowing that at the first stirrings below, I'll go down, apologize for staying so long, and take my leave. Still, in the classic paradox of the hangover, the longer I lie in bed and the more still I keep myself, the worse I feel. So I close my eyes and sleep. Soon, Bud is at my door, knocking gently, urging me awake the way my son does before I drive him to school. "How you doing?" Bud says, gentle and funny. "You ready to go eat some biscuits?"

In the kitchen, Daly sorts papers, ticks off the day's tasks—the calls he must make, the faxes he needs to catch. His day is a series of memos to the self. When I lumber in, he wearing the same shirt from the night before, signing photos, and drinking water from an olive-tinted glass. He shakes the cramp from his hand and looks me up, then down. "You ever had chocolate gravy?"

Bud moans, revs the engines a bit. "Oh, yeah! The gravy. You gotta love the gravy."

Daly smiles. "You gotta come over to have some of MamaLou's chocolate gravy."

"Oh, MamaLou," Bud says. He slides his hands in his pockets and smiles. "Nothin' like the chocolate gravy."

We walk across the patch of lawn that separates John Daly from his parents. A hundred yards, tops. Daly trudges ahead of me like a golfer skillfully outpacing his caddie, step for step. Bud hangs next to me. The air edges on frost, but the ground has give. It's cool, and the morning has a sting of pine sap. Daly points up at the mountain, then back to his house. "I'm putting in some drainage here. There's water coming off that mountain all the time. We'll have to put something in here—tiles, I guess." He pauses there and looks back at his house, dim and muddy in the early light. "My brother can do that. He knows what he's doing."

MamaLou is not surprised to see me. She pulls me right into the kitchen and offers me a seat. "You boys have fun last night?" she asks. There's no chiding in her voice, not even a hint of reproach.

Bud lights a cigarette. "Shanae was singing."

"That girl," Daly's mother says, "can really sing."

Daly's father enters. It's 7:50. He holds his hand out, as if he'd been expecting company. "Pleasure," he says. He is barrel-chested and neatly dressed with a name tag on. JIM DALY, it reads. COLDWELL BANKER.

John Daly watches it all from the end of the island. "This countertop is looking good, Mama." He runs his finger along the edge. "They just installed this," John tells me. "Granite."

Bud sways from side to side, nursing his hangover a bit. "MamaLou, I need a Diet Coke. Have you got a Diet Coke?"

She brings him his Diet Coke and opens one for John without asking. She is a tiny woman, and she moves tentatively in her own kitchen, as if something might fall at any time. Daly's father stands at the stove and makes himself a bowl of watery oatmeal. Everyone except me is smoking.

"You don't have to eat that," MamaLou says to me, referring to the oatmeal. "I have breakfast all ready for you boys. You ever had chocolate gravy?"

"No, ma'am," I say. "Never have."

This much I know: You open a biscuit with your fingers. You lay both halves on the plate, insides facing up. You spoon on the gravy.

You fork it into small pieces and you eat.

Chocolate gravy is like hot pudding, only better, and I'm mopping it up, as they say in Arkansas. Bud is moaning, saying all the right things to the cook. "MamaLou, there ain't nothin' like this." He crumbles two hard planks of bacon onto his chocolate-covered biscuit and whistles. He points a fork at me. "You can't get this just anywhere."

John laughs. "That's right. Only in Dardanelle." He has his yellow sunglasses on, hat knocked back on his head, sweatjacket zipped to the nipple. He looks as if he's ready to go, but there doesn't appear to be anywhere *to* go.

His father pipes in. "You boys practice at all yesterday?"

They shoot each other a look. "It was a good day," Bud says. "We were working all day."

Daly smiles, waves a cigarette at me. "We had to get old Tom here through his interview." They echo the old games of adolescence: the furtive glance, the snicker. We laugh as if we've put something over on his parents. But Daly's parents aren't biting. "We'll get out there today," John says.

"You want some more bacon?" MamaLou asks me.

"No," I say, "but thank you just the same." I sip my Diet Coke.

"You have to be curious about John," she says. Smoke twists off the end of her cigarette and hangs above the table. I grab one of John's Marlboros and light it, though I haven't smoked since I was nineteen, and nod that I am.

She starts the way mothers often do: "He's a good boy and he knows it," she says. "But you have to work a little to make others know it. He loves his mother. The two of us spend time together.

Oh, yes, we do. We'll drive off, over to Tunica to play the riverboats. I just love the slots. He gets all that from me. The gambling, anywise. I have no problem telling you that I lost three hundred dollars on my last visit." She pauses there to let it sink in. "The rest of it—the golf and drinking, anyway—that came right from his father's blood, I suspect."

Daly looks out the window to the edge of the course. "You want to play?" he asks me. I do and I don't. It's a nice day, and the course is empty, set against a mountain and lined with the barren winter trees. But I have a plane to catch, no clubs, and a hangover working. I decline. "You should come out to the coast," John says. "We should play."

His mother encourages me. "You should play. You should go out there and play. He would love to have you out there," she says, the whole thing sounding like a sleepover—which, so far, is exactly what it has been.

"What's not to like?" Bud says. "Spending time with John."

"Finish the article," John says, hammering his cigarette out on a saucer. "And we'll just play." I promise him I will and ask for another Diet Coke.

"Shoot," Bud says. "Palm Springs. John Daly. What's not to like in that?"

A week later, I meet him at the thirteenth green on one of the PGA West courses, which snakes through a stack of condominiums like an East Coast bus route. We've both forgotten our promises. John can't play—the PGA wants a photo shoot that day—and I'm still finishing the article.

It feels like years ago, that shiny night in western Arkansas. In the interim, John and Shanae have driven across the country in his van. He never flies, not when he can help it.

"Big Tom," he says.

"Is that Long John Daly?" I say. We grab each other by the arms and laugh. "I wish we could play," he says. "But I have to practice today."

So we talk. We're good at that by now. He lights a cigarette, holds it in his right hand, and chips balls with his left. His caddie, whom he calls Wedge, hangs in the background, collecting balls from the area around the green. Daly hits thirty balls without ever using both hands. Every ball stops within three feet of the cup. This is the short game everyone forgets when they talk about John Daly. The balls nudge one another closer and closer to the cup.

He calls to his caddie after holing one from forty feet. "Wedge," he says, "Bud got Tom pretty drunk the other night."

Wedge just hums. He won't talk to the press, not for anything.

"I wanted to read you a lead paragraph I'm considering," I say. I'm figuring this will piss him off. That he'll shut down when he hears it, and then I'll pack up and go home. In my own clever way, I've waited until I got everything I needed before reading this—not that I'm under any obligation to read him anything.

I give him my first line: "John Daly is going to die."

He shrugs, continues chipping. "He'll run his car into a tree or his liver will fail." I press on, reading him the full paragraph. It is—at this moment, anyway—an absolute keeper. "Someone will beat him to death with a two-by-four. He'll drown in his pool. You know the list: Lung cancer. Bad kidneys. Heart disease. He's going to die.

He's wired that way."

Daly shrugs. He leans on his pitching wedge and looks at me. "You gonna say I'll win another major?"

"I was, thinking you probably will. I'll find a way to say it."

He looks back toward the clubhouse, having forgotten to tell me one way or the other if he can live with my idea about his dying. I'm ready to tell him my next paragraph, about how he's going to live before he dies. But he's off the green, heading to the cart. He waves me along.

"I'm hungry," he says. "You ready to eat?"

Greed and Giving Up

{ PART III }

23   Let's Play Two

GOLF IS A GAME OF GREED. YOU COME TO THE course wanting more, you play the course wanting more, and you tend to leave it that way, too. Land. Water. Time. Greed. These are the elements, bud. Throw in a shitty wooden boat and you have a Greek tragedy.

Now look at me. I'm playing Rio Hondo, a harsh little track in a harsh little town called Downey, in southern California, with my boy Quinn, a friend from college. The day is half done, the sky a tilt of blue, the golf going poorly, so I'm wiring the last hole, trying to hold it together for a big finish. It's almost noon, we're bearing down on the clubhouse, and I'm betting that he wants more.

Keep in mind that we have played eighteen holes. It's been a full morning, with the usual menagerie of golf adventure: bogies, pure shots, skulls. Ho-hum. Like I said, not so good. But Quinn, my old friend, has game now, and he's stung me for about thirty dollars. My arms hurt, my back is stiff, and my putter isn't working. Still, I have nothing ahead of me except the Father, Son, and Holy Ghost of empty business travel: the room, the bar, and the rental car. While Quinn has places to be, appointments to keep, phone calls to make, I'm guessing I've got him figured. Any moment now, he's going to suggest another eighteen.

Truth is, nobody questions how often you eat out, and nobody cares about the frequency of your museum visits, how many movies you allow yourself in a month, how many books you read, or how much time you spend on a treadmill.

But play enough golf and you're guaranteed to find people who'll give you shit about it. They'll ask you about it again and again. In fact, over time, you come to realize that your golf really pisses these people off. "Too much time," they'll tell you, invoking the great modern myth of how busy we all are. "How can you afford to spend that much time on it? I can't afford to waste five hours."

Occasionally, though, someone will come along to defend your right to play a full round of golf a couple of times a week. Somehow, he or she sees and appreciates the elegant pace of the game, the blessed disrespect for time, the delicate framing of the world that occurs in a round of golf. He or she respects the good that eighteen holes can do.

But even so, no one roots for you to play thirty-six. No one. Not your spouse, not your children, not even your regular foursome, unless they happen to be there with you when it happens. Telling someone to go play thirty-six is like pulling for someone to eat the seventy-two-ounce porterhouse in one sitting, no doggie bag. People consider it huge, gluttonous, galling.

A round of golf takes half a day. Hit some balls beforehand, drink some beers and poke at a basket of pretzels afterward, and you might get on toward dinnertime. But two rounds unfolds the day, drags the game from the creepy light of dawn toward the wither of twilight. Depending on how you look at it, you're either sacrificing the day or making a sacrifice to the day.

The moment has to be right. The course must be relatively uncrowded, and the company, good. The weather, too. The day must yawn ahead of you. But the second tour through a course is worth it. Thirty-six holes is the ultimate indulgence, golf's saltiest pleasure, reminding you with every step of both the muscle of the game and the scale of a single turn of the planet.

So, back at Rio Hondo, Quinn turns to me and says the number. "Thirty-six?" He doesn't have to say anything else. I'm with him. I want more.

We swing into the clubhouse and sign on to play as a foursome with a Japanese couple. There are forty minutes before our tee time, so we sit. Time passes. Quinn takes out a cell phone; he has appointments to cancel. We pass Motrin and bust chops. It's a good place to be—a clean, well-lighted clubhouse, perched in those minutes between one round and the next, our carts outside, already loaded.

Playing thirty-six holes is about the only acceptable argument for golf carts there is, because walking thirty-six is a nasty business. A round of golf is about a six-mile walk, so two rounds is like walking from one end of Manhattan to the other, carrying a bag of clubs and wearing a pair of khakis and shoes with knobby little spikes on the bottom. By the end, you feel as damp, nasty, and scratchy as a horse blanket.)

We get off the first hole at about 1:30. The Japanese couple speaks no English, but the husband has a tight swing, and his wife simply doesn't miss. Quinn rips his tee shot, and I smooth mine to a good lie about ten yards short of his. There are no nerves, no jitters.

In the second round, you lean on every shot, a bit more secure in your sense of what's ahead, of what the play is, of where your swing is in general. The first time through on any course, every hole is a kind of dreamy construction that you play by instinct and view like photographs. On the second go-round, you're no longer balancing seeing the course against playing the course. No kinks, no rust, no worries in the swing. You're just playing. And for a time, you're better than you were that very morning.

At the twenty-ninth hole, the light in the sky changes; Quinn and I double the bet. The Japanese guy has strung together seven pars. His wife is riding now, not playing at all. We're standing near a chain-link fence that runs along a spillway, waiting for the group in front of us. On the other side of the fence, three Mexican teenagers stand with their arms folded. One of them flashes a crowbar. Quinn looks at them, then at the fairway. The Japanese guy takes practice swings. "California is fucked-up," Quinn says.

When I get to the tee, I realize how tired I am. I take a sigh, tee the ball, and lace a low fade to the right center of the fairway. My game is just out of reach now. I can feel my swing somewhere in me, beneath the achy wrist and the sore back, but it is resisting me. I can feel how the rest of it will go. There won't be another really solid drive, there will be a struggle to string good shots together, there will be one tremendously long putt and several short misses. All the while, I will know that I could be playing better, that I have lost what little touch I had.

So when I turn back to the cart and catch Quinn looking at his watch, why do I not want to quit right then and there? Because I know that when Quinn looks at his watch, he's not wondering how long this will all take, he's wondering how many hours of sunlight are left. "You know," Quinn says, nodding to the Japanese woman, "if she's done for the day, we could play through and really make some time on these last few holes."

"That's true," I say.

"It's only four o'clock," Quinn says.

"Is that all?" I say.

"You want to get through and play a little more?" he asks.

That's when I tell him who I am, what I am. I'm a golfer. I'm greedy. Sure, I want just a little more. I always do.

(24) The Last Manservant

FOR THE PAST MONTH, I'VE BEEN CHANNEL-flipping past a scene in an old movie in which a Philadelphia blue blood gets a straight-razor shave from his butler. This is one of those scenes that you stumble on again and again, caught, as it is, in the cruel rotation of the off-brand movie channel. After a minute or so, I move on. Why not? It all seems so far away, a mere relic of days long gone, when money ruled and success was measured in possessions. That, and I have to check my E*Trade account on my WebTV. About the fifth time I landed on this scene, I began to wonder what a butler would cost. A lot, I figured. I mean, they must have to go to a butler academy or something. They must need to be board certified. Finding a butler would be no slim trick. Expensive, too. Still, there had to be a low-end butler, a kind of "guy Friday," one who drives you, dusts occasionally, grills effectively, and irons your khakis in front of *SportsCenter* while you sleep off a champagne hangover. The kind of guy who'd hand you the right bottle of wine, find the bon mot for your upcoming toast, who'd look past your various failures the way the rest of us ignore a mid-day drizzle. What would that cost? I had it figured at 65K plus three weeks of paid vacation and a 401(k). Bottom end. Health insurance, too. And a private room. Furnished.

So, like most people, I flipped past this scene, on to the other channels of consumption and desire. But it occurred to me that, as always, I was already getting a vision of what I wanted from my time on the golf course. While I couldn't have a butler, I could afford myself a caddie. In fact, I could pretty much afford the very best caddie. Not every day, mind you—who wants that, really?—but often enough to know what it's all about. Maybe this guy wouldn't shave me while I plow through *The Wall Street Journal*, but a good caddie might hand me a five-iron and give me a nod at just the right moment, at the downwind end of a 190-yard approach, at 3:15 on a Wednesday, a day when we both should be working and we both know it. Only he is and I'm not.

No human relationship is so thoroughly one-way, so rightfully self-ish, so unapologetically exploitative as that between you and your caddie. The caddie is the last manservant—expert, dignified, sun-baked. He puzzles you out. He examines your swing with the mod-est respect most brokers give to T-bills. But then he experiments, shaving yards here, adding a club there, until he knows you well enough to hand you the right stick without speaking, to make the distance without being asked, to urge you with just a glance to fin-ish your swing.

Now, you might show this to a female friend, who might read it and say, "How very male! To want a relationship that's one-way, in which the one person exists solely to anticipate the needs of the other." To which I reply, Manicurist! Hairstylist! Therapist! Masseuse! Everyone wants this, a relationship that is oddly sexual in the way familiarity and anticipation are the core issues by day's end and regret perches itself at the eighteenth, when you hand your caddie fifty bucks and he moves on to the next John Doe.

Truth be told, the caddie is a rare pleasure, replaced at public and private courses alike by the squirrelly whine of the golf cart, with its drink holders, sun visor, and global-positioning device. But the golf cart is a lame companion—it is bumpy, silly looking, and as grimly able as a Mormon. Play from a cart and you come to ignore the space between the shots. Play from a cart and you're constantly jogging back for another club. The truth is, play from a cart and no one gets much of a look at your butt-ugly swing. With a cart, you can run and you can hide.

The caddie doesn't have any cup holders. Hold your own damn cup. As for global positioning, no one on the golf planet knows his position better than a good caddie. Just ask him. He'll tell you in yards, or he won't tell you at all. He'll watch you, all right. He'll even pass judgment, but unlike most people, if you ask him, he'll tell you what he thinks.

Sadly, not many clubs have caddies. You can try to train your own. I did. I asked my neighbor's son, a skinny kid who mows my lawn, to carry my bag one Thursday. "There's twenty bucks in it," I said.

He shrugged. Our whole relationship seems to be about me handing him twenties.

I drove him up to the course, went to the back of my car, and slid on my shoes. He peered into the trunk, sniffing at the bag, staring at my cache of new sleeves. I tied my shoelaces and turned toward the clubhouse. When the kid started after me, he did so without the bag. "You have to carry my clubs," I said. He looked hurt.

He carried the bag up to the clubhouse and dropped it loudly on the cart path. I cringed. "Stand it up," I said. "That's your job." He apologized and put his hands in his pockets.

My partners hadn't arrived yet, so I decided to play a few holes to warm up. I slaughtered my first drive, and as I left the box the kid said, "Jesus!"

Good kid! I had nutted it. Behind me, he had tucked the bag behind his back. This had potential. We came over the crest of the first fairway and my ball was nowhere to be seen. "Jesus!" the kid said again.

I smiled. "I hammered it," I said. "It will be up ahead."

When I looked back, I realized he hadn't been talking about my shot. Now he was carrying the bag under his arm, like someone lugging a box of rugs through customs. "This thing is heavy!" he said.

I was about 130 yards out. This was his first test. "A nine, maybe," I said.

He started pawing through the bag. "Yeah, you have one right here."

I waited, but he wasn't handing me anything. He had his hands in his pockets again. I rattled around and grabbed my nine. Then I knocked it stiff to the back edge of the green. Another good shot. When I turned back to him, the kid was standing in the trees, twenty yards away, his back turned to the shot. He held his arm up in triumph. "Hey," he said. "I found a lighter!"

It went like that for three holes. I'd flip him a ball on the green, looking for a wipe-down, and he'd pocket it and say, "Thanks." When I asked him for my putter, he said, "Maybe you should carry that one yourself. You use it a lot."

He was done. I fired him and shouldered my own bag when my friends showed up. I realized that the problem was simple: He hadn't lived; he'd never had sex; he'd never even begun to know what it is to anticipate the needs of another person. He had no idea how to charm, to serve, to challenge someone. I could teach him the game; I could not teach him the craft.

When you do it right, you arrive at a course twenty minutes early. The caddies huddle near a shed, in the semicircle of the tobacco ritual. The caddie master throws someone your way, a guy who limps out, holsters your bag, and reliably leads you to the practice green. He talks like a bartender and looks like a barfly.

You introduce yourself. You're Mike. He's Andy. You tell a joke. He laughs. He begins his work without your noticing, reordering your clubs, taking inventory of your supply of balls. You putt. He watches like an uncle, intent and curious, relaxed and ready to help. You might turn to him for advice or stare straight past him to the clubhouse. It's all the same to him, for, later, you will pay him.

You can hire a guy to fix your Saab, but he's loyal to the problem, to the circuitous solution, not to you. You can hire a guy to clean your house, but he'll just get pissed when you leave the can of cashews overturned on the glass table again. You might have an accountant, but the odds are he's telling you what you *can't* do with your money. These people are banking on your inabilities. Screw them. What you need is a team player, someone who understands what you can do. You need a caddie.

25 The Right to Privacy

LET'S OPEN WITH A CUT TO THE PARKING LOT of a good public golf course near you. It's Saturday, so things are crammed, cars packed in so tightly that the lot overflows onto the state highway. Men are leaning against fenders, smoking cigarettes, sipping huge plastic drink cups full of Diet Mountain Dew. The practice green, jammed up against the tractor shed ever since they expanded the parking lot last summer, is a forest of khaki. There are two guys wearing jeans. And another two throwing a Frisbee near the driving range, which like every other aspect of the facility is trammeled by small sets of thirty-two year-old men who have decided to take up golf at long last. They stand in small circles, talk loudly, and, oh yeah, they have also decided to start smoking cigars. Today. Just now. They spent four bucks apiece!

Cut to you. You called for a tee time three weeks ago. You were squeezed in just behind the regular fivesome of retires from the old

IBM plant. When the kid told you this on the phone, he clearly meant it to sound comforting. Now you shoulder through the masses, set your bag in alongside the bag stand, since it is as full-up as a Motel 6, twist your way past the cigar smokers, through their cloud, into the pro shop, which is 880 feet of retail overpopulation. The pro is weary, windblown, and utterly unconcerned. He hasn't seen a real player since he walked off his junior college team back in '88. He reloads the freezer with Nutty Buddies as you check in.

You know this sort of course. Wickedly quirky, perhaps possessed of a vaguely glorious history, but in your lifetime it stood as no more than a sleepy municipal track—until recently, when it was given a top-thirty ranking by *Golf Digest*. Now everyone knows it. And with everyone on the Eastern Seaboard taking up golf at this particular moment in history, this sort of course is both the victim and the beneficiary of the boom. There's nothing wrong with it. Everybody should play golf. It is the greatest game, ancient and wondrous. Better men than I can testify to that. Yes. It is without parallel. And one more person discovering its pleasures, learning the muscular comfort of nutting a drive or the sheer, almost obscene, pleasure of stiffing a pin—why, these new citizens only strengthen the game.

But they jam up the parking lot, too.

Cut to the private club. Observe the smooth unrushed curves of the driveway. The parking lot—empty. The bag stand—yours. The pro shop—huge and resplendent. The patio—elegant tablecloths! The course—particular, sure, but most important, empty and untaxed, empty as the day is long, both fore and aft.

I have friends who don't like clubs, who see them as overly exclusive, isolating, elitist, earth-sprung from the blue blood of nineteenth-century industrialists. To them, any club that calls itself what it is—a club—represents an irritation, an offense, a rift in the moral fabric. They won't even think about joining. I get that. I used to be one of them, frankly. You know, I didn't want to be in any club that would have me as a member. It's a familiar sentiment.

However, that was before I got stuck on a local nine playing in a foursome with three college kids who retreated to smoke a clandestine one-hitter each time I teed off. And before I was forced to hit range balls between two concrete walls into the front side of a mountain at a public track in Ohio. Before I hit behind my first fivesome. Before I watched two teenagers race golf carts up and down a par-five while I was pitching to the flag. Before, in short, I suffered the lion's share of indignities that public golf courses present.

So I joined. I had just grown impatient and old. I expected things from the game, from my game, and I decided that enough was enough—enough with the cigars and the blue jeans, enough with the long lines, enough with the people cutting from one fairway to the next to chase down their ducks. Enough. I'm old. You might say I appear to be a grumpy old man. But I need some decorum. I need a sense of order from the world around me. The private club provided it.

At its best, joining a good golf club is like buying into small-town living—at a really classy small town. Everyone knows each other. Everyone seems to respect the rules. Like any small town, it comes replete with its bullies, and its sheriffs, and its dowdy citizenry. You get all this and a little elbow room, to boot. Everything in a private club should be controlled and uncrowded. At first, this is the club's greatest asset. Legroom in the lounge. Storage room in the locker. And when you're on the course, voila, you get generous helpings of the game's two best watchwords: pace and space. Room to breathe.

Eventually everything—every nuance and rhythm of the clubhouse, of the course, even of the people you play with by chance—becomes second nature. After awhile you engage in a sort of secret language with the course, one that is all your own. After all, the course is, in some ways, yours.

In this way the game extends itself and expands. By joining a private club, you buy into a whole new kind of game, a game where playing offers you a set of challenges that are both familiar in that you face them often, and thrilling in that they are so distinctly yours. You understand the fourth green. You know to use an extra club from the fairway on seven. You understand the landing area at fifteen. It is, in the end, all about you.

Now there is nothing more lovely than a public course on a sunny, uncrowded day. Let's face it. Golf is golf. And you can't begrudge anyone—neither the chop or the slicer—his weekly chance at glory. Everyone deserves to play. So long as they play fast and fair and don't turn the whole outing into some kind of weird six-hour-long cross between a three-legged race and a keg party right in front of your eyes. All too often, this is the case at the public course, where manners are generally enforced by a doddering ranger rather than by institution itself.

The truth is, there comes a point where you want to get past the trivialities of time, where you want to concentrate on your game, to know the golf course as a sort of constant. The private club is marvelously predictable in this way.

The foot traffic at private courses is a different sort of business. Crowds are rarely an issue. The crowds at public courses are too happenstance, too affected by the trade winds of a good economy, just as are they prone to fall victim to the nor'easters of an economic slowdown. When things are good, everyone plays. When things are bad, public golf falters. Upkeep slips, rules change, standards side.

A club—a good one—perseveres. The golf course is maintained, held steady by the membership. The greens remain topgrade, the tee boxes, level. Even the iced tea is notable.

I often sneak off to my club during lunch and play four holes amidst the sleepy foursomes who populate the course during the week. It is then that I am struck by how the game I play has been shaped by the club to which I belong.

I try to play a polite, undemanding game when I am on my own four-hole circuit. From the moment I tee off, I keep one eye ahead and one eye behind, so I can step out of the way of any group. At my club, the rule is singletons always give way. If there's anything that membership in a club reminds you of, it's that—a rule's a rule.

I adore the pure quietude of my club, the sense that I am far from the beltway, even more distant from my office, with each step advancing into a state of calm. There is no whir of golf carts surrounding me. No churning driving range to distract me. Only the familiar greenskeeper passing this way and that, atop his stolid John Deere, giving me a quarter-wave and a nod. From the moment I hit the first ball I do not speak, not even under my breath. And in this I have learned to borrow the quiet of my club and visit it upon my game.

Now I see people I know, and I will speak to them. Familiar faces are another of the great pleasures of the private club. I love to see my friends—the basketball coach, the restaurateur, the real-estate agent, the three stocks guys, the woman who runs the radio station—and I always stop to chat. They offer to let me join them, and sometimes I do, but most often I press forward into the silence and the space. I find my way back into the world that I have paid for, where the game is uncluttered and spare. Me. Some grass. The ball.

Now before I get too Zen on you, let me add that I love the club sandwich at my club. Always rye toast! They never even ask! I mean, the private club does offer some pleasures I associate with my more base instincts toward comfort and respect. My pro knows my game, though it is not worth even looking at. He knows my name, my kids' names, what sort of car I drive, what I do for a living, how poorly I play in the rain. He knows I hate jokes and I don't want to talk politics. He cuts me real deals on the clubs I buy from him. He even sends me a Christmas card. I even adore the reliable cadre of kids who staff the pro shop, who always seem happy to see me, who stock the ice cream novelties in the back room where no one can see them.

I like the fish fries. I like the umbrella they put over the chairs. I appreciate the pool, if only for my sons' sake. I like the fact that they grill burgers during scrambles and that I can charge drinks at the golf cart. I will even occasionally go to a dance, just to get a taste of a life I associate with long summers in the Poconos.

So I'm not pure. I appreciate the whole package. I buy in at every level. I like it private, a bit closed off. I read those words and have a hard time believing that I wrote them. I am, above all, a social guy. But the older I get, the more I feel left out by the world. I am forty-three. Music, fashion, technology. I was locked out of these things years ago. In some ways, I left behind any hope of getting on top of them. I pushed back. And so now, in my private club, I push back yet again. And I'm done apologizing for it.

Robert Frost said, "Good fences make good neighbors." And in some ways I've always considered this Frost's meanest sentiment, since it asks for separation, suggests a world in which we are strengthened by that which divides us.

But the old guy was right. The fence that a club puts up is just enough to balance the game for its members, to hold it steady for their enjoyment. Sure, some people are outside looking in. But it's always that way with golf. The game itself is a kind of fence. Even when you're standing on the tee box at the most crowded muni in the world, there are still mooks driving by you on the interstate wishing they were on the course, at the tee, ready to play. They are looking in, too, over the fences. Hungry for some game. Public or private, when you're playing golf, you're in—and everyone who isn't playing is out.

Admit it. You're in, and you're happy.

26 The Marathon

SOMETIMES IT'S HARD TO ARGUE that golf is a sport. A sport is work and sweat, a measure of pain and competition. Golf has too much in the way of beer and benches, carts and cool breezes, to make anyone believe that you're really working out. Arguing that golf is a sport requires real imagination when 60 percent of your dry-cleaning bill is devoted to keeping a crisp seam on your golf pants and your polo shirts wrinkle-free.

Still, no one would argue that three rounds of golf isn't a workout, and when you've done that you start to understand where the golf muscles reside—and that those muscles can fight back in the same tweaks and twinges you remember from jayvee football practice.

So you might argue that you have to push yourself to make golf a sport, and three rounds is pushing it, to be sure. But what about something like five rounds in a day? Or seven? What about something really crazy, like ten rounds in a day? Wouldn't that reclassify things a bit? Wouldn't that throw things into the realm of ironmen, marathoners, triathletes? Wouldn't something like 180 holes in fifteen hours of daylight throw the game/sport question right out the window?

The only way to find out is to try. The only place you can try without getting booted by rangers, divorced by your spouse, or committed by your doctor is *Washington Golf Monthly's* Golf Decathlon, a charity fundraiser for Special Olympics and an event with a strong foothold as an unquestionably unwise challenge to the foolhardy.

When you tell someone you're off to play ten rounds of golf, it strikes them as at least a week's work. They ask, "When do you get back from Ireland?" When you tell them you're playing ten rounds of golf in one day, they ask simpler questions, things like, "Are you stupid?"

Some people want to know if there are enough hours in the day to play ten rounds. They start to calculate on cocktail napkins, dividing the sunlight into little wedges of time, each representing hole. Once you've done a decathlon, you can save them a little math. "Five minutes a hole," you tell them. No breaks. No burgers at the turn. No milling around the clubhouse between rounds. Five minutes—no more, no less. You watch as they turn this over in their minds. These guys are your friends. You play with them all the time. Some of them spend five minutes on a single shot, deciding between a four-iron and a five-wood. They wouldn't stand a chance in a decathlon.

Maybe they just aren't athletes.

Washington Golf Monthly's Third Annual Golf Decathlon began on a clear morning this past July at Woodmere Club in Prince George County. Fifteen intrepid golfers, many of them veterans of previous decathlons, set out to do the deed once again in the Special Olympics fundraiser. We hit our first ball at 5:30 AM.

By itself, teeing off this early falls into a recognizable band of golf normalcy. I recall that as my group (there were only two of us) made the turn it was 6:25 AM. Oddly, this didn't seem strange to me either. I'm used to rising early and playing quickly on courses still empty before the midday rush. What really marked the day as different was that my playing partner fretted at the turn that we were playing slowly. "We're five minutes behind," he said, "and this is only the first round."

By nine o'clock we were just into our second round and I was starting to feel cocky. I'd opened with a serviceable round and followed that with an eighty-two, with a triple at the last. I felt loose, limber, and relatively cool. My feet were just a little wet from the morning dew, but otherwise I was all systems go. "Let's pick up the pace," I told my partner. I felt sure I was about to go low.

What's hard for me to fathom is what happened next. Not directly—not the next hole, which was surely just another hole in a blinding, seemingly endless series—but presently, in the coming hours during which the heat rose, the pace stiffened, and the day unfolded like something grotesquely out of scale, a circus tent pulled from a child's backpack.

First, during a throwaway round, a ninety-two, I approached a given par-five for the third or fourth time and found that I couldn't remember the hole at all. "Is this a par-five?" I said to my driver, my editor, Bill Kammenjar.

He looked at me like I was crazy. "This is the fourth time you've seen it," he said. "It's going to be the same every time."

Still, no matter how hard I looked, I found that I couldn't remember it, that it didn't register. I might as well have been a pioneer staring at the western horizon for the very first time. "Man," I said. "I need some water."

Sometime later, an hour, maybe two—in a decathlon time waffles and confounds, so who can say really?—I found that I was back at the same hole. Since I'd been there last, I'd filled up two score cards, consumed eleven bottles of water, rolled in two birdies, wolfed down a sandwich on the run, lost two balls, pulled a hamstring, and developed a blister the size of a quarter on my gloveless hand. I stood on the same tee box and looked out. "Is this a par-five?" I said again. This time Bill only laughed and handed me a driver. "Just hit," he said, "You'll only see it four more times."

I can recall very little of what followed. I can't say why. It may have been the heat, or the sheer drumming repetitiveness. Surely the five-minute-a-hole pace did me no good. But soon I lost any sense of what the game was. My irons got longer. My putts stayed short of the hole. I found that I didn't want to watch the ball in flight any more, even on my best shots. At one point I hit a seven-iron from 155 yards and as I approached the cart Bill asked me, "Did you get into it?"

I snapped at him: "I don't give a damn." And just then a roar went up from the green. The ball had dropped like a rock on the edge of the hole and settled four feet from the pin. When I got to the green they showed me the ball's mark, pressed into the curl of the cup, and congratulated me.

"Best shot of the day," my partner said. I proceeded to miss the putt. I didn't care. I didn't care. I didn't care. No one did.

So it was. I lost myself in the late rounds of the golf decathlon. The sun skidded across the sky, and people began to get nervous. Groups started playing to one another. It felt to me that a sort of chaos had descended onto the world. My back tightened. My feet were so soggy I thought they might slip their skin. My forehead burned.

All of which is to say that I did have fun at points. I just can't remember what points they were, or the specific context in which they occurred. We all, both carts, driver and player alike, laughed a lot. At one point, Bill dubbed the event "The U.S. Open of Stupidity." As groups played through, or by, us, there was much talk of "Never again!" from the golfers who passed.

Still, as the final hour of sunlight approached and it became certain that we would, indeed, finish, I did feel the full flush of accomplishment begin to take over. Ten rounds. Fifteen hours. It was something I could tell to my grandchildren, brag about to my friends. As we crested the last hole for the tenth time, the light had yet to fail. I got the sense that I could dig deeper, that I could find a reserve. I leaned into a five-iron, and it was all but done. As I approached the green, I realized that I could keep going if called upon, that I could eek out a few more holes if someone needed me to. Oh, why not? You can play a game any day, but sometimes you just gotta be a sport.

(27) The Offseason

IT'S A FRIDAY IN MIDWINTER, AND WE'RE ONE hour into our regular poker game, once around the table with a goofy anaconda. Someone has insisted that we listen to *Surrealistic Pillow* by Jefferson Airplane, and I can't stand that shit, so I'm just trying to block it out while I try to decide whether to commit high or low. I have to pass three cards to my right. The fish always sits to my right. I take one look. The guy works his eyebrows like an antique sewing machine while gnawing on a pretzel rod. He's the new guy, and he plays like a new steel bucket: round, loud, and shiny. Still, I haven't won a hand yet. The song is "Plastic Fantastic Lover," and the ante is a buck. Outside, the wind is dragging through the trees like a sickle.

In my part of the planet, it is cold. Too cold. Far too cold for golf. Sure, there are places where men are hitting buckets and buckets of range balls, even at this very minute. But this is January in the

American Midwest; the weather's dodgy; the ground's frozen. Ice has been hanging in huge spears from my gutters for three weeks now. Forget golf. We're playing poker.

I hand the fish a made hand. Three eights. I'm going low, and I might as well get him halfway home to a shitty full house. The fish looks at the cards one at a time. When he sees the third eight, he almost swallows the pretzel rod sideways. At the other end of the table, someone says of the music, "This is Jerry Garcia here. All through this part."

And the answer comes, "Just pass me my goddamn cards."

The regular poker crew is a dappled thing, speckled and sundry, populated by wheezers, cranks, and smart guys. Each of them—every single slob at the table—assumes he is the one to fear, the straw that stirs the drink. Because the truth is, every man everywhere is certain he can play poker, too, or he could if he had to. In some semipeaceful, postapocalyptic nation-state, men know that they might bank on their wits, move from town to town, jump from one card game to the next. Men consider poker a basic skill, a simple matter of concentration. To be fair, these guys might actually be players. Then again, they could be fish.

My usual group of seven involves three regulars—me, my golf buddy Wayne, and David, the perpetual host whose kitchen is so familiar to me now, it feels like a vacation house—and three semi-regular satellites—journalists, classics professors, lawyers, bankers, poets—who are only as regular as their enthusiasm for the game. They come and go, blowing in on spare cash and the nagging certainty that tonight might just be their night. The seventh seat goes to a fish, the new blood, the kind of guy who wanders into the game because he's heard about it and says he played big-money hands in college and he's even been thinking about entering the World Series of Poker, not now, but in, like, twenty years, after he's had some time to work on his game. The game starts at 8:30. The fish is usually on the dock by 11:00.

Poker is a heavy pleasure, so rife with ceremony, smoke, and language that it could be considered Catholic. As the night unfolds, we name one another. The civil-rights lawyer is christened Big Daddy because he'll bet only the monster hands. The fat education professor becomes Bizarro when he misdeclares on three straight hands. The names are only for the table. Everywhere else, these guys are John and Bill. But when the game begins, they are who they were the last time we played, never mind the in-between. They're poker players. We all are. Big Daddy, Bizarro, Smokehouse, Joey the Scent, Wayne-O, the Lothario, and the Hungarian.

A game of poker is textured almost entirely by chatter. Games are invented, rehashed, and renamed. In poker, as in golf, slow players kill the game. The night dwindles with each hand, just as the golf course shrinks in front of the golfer. Losers sometimes sulk and winners sometimes gloat, and everyone, before long, is humbled. And in those tremendous moments, when luck raises a flag for someone in particular, there are roars.

Poker. Golf. These are small doings, played at the end of workweeks for drinking money and the cost of a little time. Still, the successes are mostly private (the full house hooked on the river card, the crisp four-iron into the wind), and the failures (busted flushes, the shanks, the failed bluffs) are almost purely public.

I recall a game several years ago when we brought in a fish, a teacher grinding the old tune—that he'd made his way through graduate school playing cards and that he was dying for a piece of the action. Things did not go well for the teacher. He called silly games loaded with wild-card combinations and burdened with moronic titles. By midnight, he was down to his last twenty, drinking everybody else's beer. At one point, caught in a showdown for a lousy pot, his hand was matched by someone holding the exact same jack-eight-six-four-three flush in a different suit. The teacher scratched his chin. "Hearts beat diamonds," he said. "It's a tiebreaker."

"The fuck it is," I said.

"Sure," the teacher said. "We always play tiebreakers." What a gimp.

"No tiebreakers," said Wayne.

We all shook our heads. No tiebreakers. The teacher protested, then grudgingly split the pot, still muttering about his scabby heart flush. "It just depends on where you play your poker, I guess," the teacher said. "And with whom."

Big Daddy sighed then. He had been the one who'd brought in this fish, and now he was losing patience. "I guess we play our poker right here," he said. "With us."

The teacher quieted down then, even clawed his way back before we closed down the table. Before he left, he shook my hand. I never saw him again.

He'd missed the point. In these games, in these gatherings, whatever certainty you possess rests in equal measure in you and in the guy across the table from you, or in you and the guy walking with you up the yoke of the fairway. You're just men, and these are just games. In many ways, you play them inside your head—holding a thought, a single piece of advice chosen from the thousands you've read or muttered or heard from a dozen yahoos in a dozen spots like this. One little mantra that—on this hand, on this morning, on this swing—will inform everything you do. On the outside, games require a sort of movement, a coordination difficult to gauge by someone who's never tried it. Poker is so simple that they play it in storerooms and boxcars, and golf is so elemental that it was invented by shepherds. Yet one game is no less ambiguous and mechanically complicated than the other. You work to master each through repetition, through failure, by paying attention to your own basic foibles. When you get even fairly good, other people think it looks really easy. And that's when they swim forward to have a go at you.

Back to Anaconda, where I throw the guy the fourth eight on the last pass and sit back to watch his ride. I'm kicking myself for not holding the eights. I've got a strong low hand, but I'm still waiting for a sure winner so I can check-raise with impunity. No matter. It's early. Soon the certainties of the evening will make themselves apparent. Wayne will hang in and steal a bunch of split pots. The Hungarian will lose track of a weak hand and bet it like a winner. The host will call low hold on his deal, and the fish will throw down his cards in disgust again and again. Someone will spill a beer. At some point, we'll hear the train rumble through town. The music will be changed again and again. Eventually, I'll snag a few hands. As things press on, we will call one another our names, and, just between us, this night will pass.

28 Losing the Bag, Losing Your Way

IN GOLF THERE ARE MANY ACTS OF PURE TRUST. You have to trust people's handicaps, since it's gauche to ask a sandbagger for his card. You have to trust your partner as he tramps around at the edge of a piney wood looking for the Strata he knocked in there on the fly. He might come up with it after all, and if he does, you have to trust that he found it fair and square. When someone reads yardage for you, you have to trust their instincts. When someone lays claim to a snowman, you have to card the eight, even though you know they played the hole at something closer to the national drinking age.

Or not.

Let's face it, these are some of the moments when trust is used, or misused, and nothing more. Trust is like a putter you've carried since you were sixteen; you know how to use it, sure, but sometimes it backfires on you.

In thinking about it, the only real moments of trust I can come up with have to do with my golf bag, which I leave at bag drops and flop onto airport conveyor belts without the least hint of how much it means to me. Leaving your golf bag with strangers is just a notch below not watching your children at the playground. The thought of it should leave you queasy, wary, and ultimately less trustful.

The golf bag is a golfer's most trusted space; it is the top drawer of all our secrets and rituals. If you think you shouldn't root around in a woman's purse, then apply that principle doubly to the golf bag, which conveys all manner of secrets, lucky charms, and health aids from place-to-place, from struggle-to-struggle, as well as the more predictable, more valuable stuff—clubs, balls, clothing. A man's golf bag is a most precise construction. In my bag, I carry a set of Ping i3s; two Cleveland wedges, one very new, one very old; three woods of varying makes and models (dependant solely upon my credit-card balance and my associated inability to squelch point-of-purchase buying sprees); and a mallet putter, which is about as much use to me as a twenty-dollar pair of dress shoes. In the pockets, I carry Band-Aids, brass ball-markers from distance courses, an acorn from Oak Hill, a pine cone from Pebble Beach, a small rock from Ballybunion, three ball mark repair tools, six Motrin, one Xanax, three gloves, forty tees, six to eight balls of every pedigree, four pencils, one pen, a copy of the rule book, an eight-foot tape measure, a rain suit, an extra pair of socks, and one tiny little bottle of Seagram's. I know where it all is, too. Don't even think about going in my bag.

Most people don't. For one thing, looking around in some-one's bag is like looking at their underwear drawer—intimate, sure, but sort of, well, gross. It's set up only for me, which makes the process of losing your bag particularly heartbreaking.

It happened to me on a flight to Las Vegas two years ago. I stood by the baggage carousel for twenty minutes after everyone else had carted off their smart little rolling bags. The carousel spun the way turntables used to, stylus bumping against the end of an album like a metronome for the clueless. It took awhile to sink in. My clubs weren't there.

At the service desk, they told me they had a line on my clubs and they were either in Bangor or Virginia Beach. Not to worry. They would have them to me by morning, they said. Besides, they added, I should be happy, since my clothes had arrived on time.

What they failed to recognize was that clothes are mere utilitarian trifles, easily replaced with a trip to the outlet mall. I could live without clothes. I was playing Reflection Bay tomorrow. I needed my sixty-degree wedge! I'd happily play in beach shorts and a T-shirt if only I could hold my own four-iron when hitting over water. Clothes! The thought of it made me sick. These people didn't understand. I was never going to see my bag again.

Yes, when morning came around, I was standing in my hotel room cursing Jimmy Carter for deregulating airlines. Or was it Ronald Reagan? In any case, I despised them both as miserable failures for letting things get to the point where the airlines could let my golf bag sit in Denver (according to their latest update) while I was about to step onto a truly great golf course without a weapon to my name. I was throwing myself at the mercy of my friend John Q., who said he had an extra bag in his garage that I could play out of for the day. Grim words on a sunny day in Nevada.

When John produced the bag from the trunk of his Caprice Classic, things made a sudden lurch for the better. It was an old leather staff bag with a broken strap, but inside it was a decent set of old Ping i2s. The woods were the usual menagerie of products once hot, now forgotten—Burner Bubbles, Orlimars, Fat Shafts. I promised myself to be optimistic, especially when the club pro lent me a Scotty Cameron putter for the day.

For a while, things went well. I was bumping along with three pars and a double to open things up, when I decided to hit the six-iron. At this point I was told the story of how John's brother had left the six-iron on a green in Scotland three years prior. "People love Pings over there," John said. "We were never going to see it again."

So I tried to ease up on a five-iron and, of course, air-mailed the green. When the ball was nowhere to be found, I tried my best not to think about where my bag was at that very moment (winging its way to Portland, I later learned), and reached into my current bag for a new ball. The pockets, alien in terms of shape and placement, confounded me, and I was unable to locate the sleeve of balls I'd bought before the round. Finally I unzipped a pocket at the bottom of the bag, stuck my hand in, and felt what seemed to be an old, dried-up glove. I knew in this moment that my hand was in utterly the wrong place at the wrong time, and I resisted the urge to pull my arm out like a schoolgirl who had just touched a garden slug. I pulled it out slowly, and found that I was holding a dead mouse. Worse, when I looked in the pocket I found a tiny litter of dead mice, zipped into the bag some months ago.

I looked up to the sky. When would my bag reach me? (Three weeks from that day, as it happened.) But the answer wasn't there.

John couldn't get over it. "Look at that," he said, looking into the pocket. "Just like a little family of mummies."

He threw me a fresh ball and told me to drop. I would unravel soon. He must have been able to see that. "Listen," he said, "don't let that bother you. You can use my clubs from here on out. Play out of my bag instead."

What he couldn't see was that that was where the trouble had started. I nodded, but I knew that day was done. The only real hope I could muster was wrapped up in my Club Glove, hurtling along its own version Magical Mystery Tour, somewhere over the west coast.

"Throw me a club then," I said.

"Which one?" John replied.

"It doesn't matter," I lied. What choice did I have? "It's your bag," I said. "I'm going to have to trust you."

$\left(29\right)$ The Meltdown

ON THIS THURSDAY, IT IS THE USUAL STORY. Here I am on the home course with two of my best boys—Wayne, a big, lanky guy whom I taught the game from scratch, and Mike, a squat, bull-strong guy who hits the ball the way Brett Hull takes wrist shots, which is to say he hammers it violently in a short, harsh cut that might be grounds for legal action in some states. We're working our usual stakes: dollars, beers, and broken balls. The components are all in place: me, them, and the distant disk of the sun inching its way across the late-afternoon sky. I've been waiting to put it all together this summer. I've been looking for my day. As we gather at the practice green, it feels like this will be it.

I open with two solid pars before pulling my tee shot left and out of bounds on the third hole. I reach in my bag, draw out another ball, and perform the very same trick once again. To make matters worse, I follow that by blocking a thin, halfhearted three-wood into a fairway bunker only 170 yards out. So here I am: Thirty minutes in, and I have doomed myself to another afternoon of unfulfilled promise, another five clicks of the clock spent scrambling, hitting unremarkable knockdowns, stumbling from one bogey to the next. I take a big, juicy sigh. My boys shoulder their bags and turn down the fairway in silence. This is my Thursday, I think. This is my fucking Thursday.

I know that moments like these are when the great players separate themselves from the fools like me. Here—lying five, walking to a ball that is on a downhill lie in wet sand, still 240 yards from home—might be precisely the place where the real men wake up. But for me, this is the moment I start questioning the whys of the game: Why did I give up pickup basketball for this? Why play golf if I can't tell whether I'm getting any better? Why didn't I at least slow down my swing? Or finish high?

More to the point, why play at all?

Mike, the hockey swinger, blows up a lot. He'll nag along for three or four holes before peeling a slice two fairways laterally. Having just picked up the game, he knows this moment well. But Mike shows no pain. He might snarl and quip, "These are the lands that I alone know well." But then he is gone, vamoose, entirely out of my par-four narrative until we magically meet at the green, where he tells me, blandly, that he is lying twelve.

Sometimes this makes me tense. Then I remember the key existential assertion of golf: Why should I care? He is not me, and I am not him. I am in this alone.

Thank God for it, too. Thank God for the singular little pencil and for the solitary tee and for the simple, silk-skinned balata resting in the center of my palm. Man against nature! Yes! Man against man. Yes! Man against himself. Alone. Of course. Day after day!

The first real sport was hunting. An individual sport: a man, a spear, a long walk. The hunter went out, trapped the animals, fought the elements, faced his fears, and brought home the kill. Man created sports, inadvertently, because he needed meat. After hunting came gathering—the second sport, a team sport if there ever was one. Handoffs and cooperation. Corn and beans. Team sports were created mostly because man needed side dishes.

Peel the skin off the game, and golf is pretty selfish. You might team up once in a while, but for the most part it's you, you, you. It is more primal than, say, pickup hoops, because of this simple truth: You are alone and nobody cares what you do.

So it's not all that dire, melting down on a Thursday afternoon in the presence of two good friends. It's part of what you risk when you play golf; any golfer might really suck on any given afternoon. You buffer yourself from this risk by banging balls into tall nylon nets, by chipping for hours in the twilight, by taking empty-handed practice swings in the office, in the parking lot, on the elevator. In this way, you balance yourself against the possibility of disaster. You grow your focus like a vine so that it fingers its way into every part of your day and occupies, front and center, your time on the course. You get better.

Still, there is a stench of inevitability about this particular meltdown. I see it in the rhythms of my friends' responses. Wayne knows to what depths I've fallen when I find myself praying for a triple bogey, when I have to get up and down from the graveyard. He looks at my lie and mutters, "Just hit it hard. That'll get you right back on track." But who really cares about a moment like this? Even if I did torch a smooth three-wood, get a good kick, and roll to a reasonable putting distance, who gives a rat's ass if I salvage a triple? No one. Not even me. Nestling your sixth shot close to the hole on a par-four is like getting a lap dance in the parking lot of a mall. The small private pleasure becomes entwined with the larger public humiliation and makes the entire pursuit—a whole set of really fun passions—frameless, ugly, and utterly unsatisfying.

Everybody strings together a run of bad holes. It happens. It is to be endured. But the true meltdown—the instant you realize you've kicked another round; the second you let yourself show your pale belly like a wretch before dropping off the map; the juncture where you check your watch, fish for your keys, and consider walking altogether—comes only once or twice a summer.

These moments of collapse are animal—panicky and intense. During the meltdown, I hate the names I call myself and the words I use; I hate my urge to explain, my dark need for sympathy above all else. I stare at the houses that line the course, hating every single resident. I stare at my ball. I stare at my hands, looking for a grip.

On this day, I take a nine. I finish the hole, place the flag in the cup, and look back. The third at my little club is a straight-ahead affair. The out-of-bounds stakes loom sure, but it's not at all tricky. I have just made a mess of it. Wayne has parred the hole, and Mike is kicking himself for missing a six-footer for a bogey. Three women are bearing down on the green, their swings long and loose, their confidence high. In silence, I thump away from the green. We're not keeping a card, but Wayne turns to me and asks, "What'd you take there?"

"That was a nine," I say.

Wayne looks confused, as if I must be mistaken. But he ponders, silently ticks back to my blundered tee shots, and nods without a word. This is our version of mercy.

At the next tee, he and Mike are off straight and true, and they leave the box to me. I think for a moment of the things I forgot between this tee and the last—the tips and the memory devices, sure, but more than these, I grope for the mindset I had twenty minutes ago. Back then, before it all fell apart, 410 yards back, I was a winner.

Screw it, I figure. Just screw it. I'll take an even bigger turn and hit the ball even harder. What more can I do to screw up an afternoon? Nothing. And when I step in, I can tell that my boys are hoping I'll rip it just this once so I'll be back on board for the rest of the ride. God bless them. And when I do, when I absolutely slaughter the ball, roping it seventy yards past them, bouncing to a flat lie, dead center of the fairway, they forget my troubles and my grumblings, as do I. with one swing, one beautiful swing, I find balance. We set out together, eyes on the horizon. This is Thursday. This is Thursday indeed.

$\left(3 0 \right)$ Why I Hate Golf

I HATE GOLF BECAUSE YOU CAN PLAY GOLF FOR TWENTY
years of Thursdays and you'll never be done with it. No matter
how well you hit your last shot, there's always one more ahead. One
more putt. One more tee shot. One more chip. One more hole. One
more tiny execution of yet another series of small, related, but otherwise unexplainable, physical acts.

There is no stopping point. No grail, no stamp, no merit
badge, no imprimatur, no certificate of mastery. Break a hundred
and you start to want ninety. Go under ninety and eighty starts to
seem realistic. Then there is the really long journey—from eighty to
seventy, which few live to tell about. Still, even those that get there,
even the pros, want a little more. Win the Grand Slam and somehow, somewhere, someone will assert that you didn't do it right.
You'll begin working on it right away.

In golf, you can't stop one day and say "There! I've done a

good job of that! Now I'll move on to tennis." You can—hell, you should—get a little better from year to year, eek out a little more from every day, from of every sequence of shots. But you don't. At least most of us don't. And if you are one of those "coffee achievers" who sets goals and achieves them, attends schools and camps and clinics, who grinds it out on the range, who sees his game notch itself up at every turn, you can never let off the gas pedal. Straighten the ball out, gain a modicum of pace on your swing, establish some mettle in your putting, but you're only a step or two further along. Your foot may be on the peddle, but you never get where you're going.

More game, more holes, more courses, more Tuesdays. The element of desire is too strong not to want more at every moment. And the desire has less to do with success—you can really suck and still want more—than with the absurd sense that everything—tip-top putting, crisp long irons, high-caliber driving—is within your reach, if you only had a little more time.

From the very moment you get to the course, you want more. More time on the green, more time to stretch, more space between you and the group ahead of you. Even if you eschew these preparatory essentials, you know you want another ten yards off that first drive. Even your best drive is only one swing away from second best. More, more, more.

Golf is all about the upgrade. Find a course you love, and some-one always wants to show you a new one just like it, or better. You're passionate about mountain golf, until you see the desert courses. You figure no course is worth a hundred bucks until there are so many three-hundred-dollar courses that the C-note seems like a bargain. Where does it end? When are you done with it for more than the day?

Some people would say: You just play. You simply go out and let the game take care of itself. You don't have to keep score. And you don't have to worry. Forget the numbers, these people say. You don't have to care in order to play.

Do not listen. They are liars, every one.

You play because you care. And you want more because the game offers it up so easily. Even as you gear your way home to the eighteenth on the best round you've ever shot, you know that there's always tomorrow, one more unlikely chance to do it just a little better.

Afterward, in the clubhouse, the last shot is a memory, the last round a story. Around the table there's always more, too—one more story, one more joke, one more tee shot relived, one more long putt—hashed and rehashed. One more bet to pay off, one more burger, one more pretzel, one more drink, one more look at the watch. You have been here for a thousand Tuesdays, and you know you will be here for at least one more.

Even as you leave, you feel pulled back. Even as the sun sets, the dawn approaches. Even as you start the car, you remember one more thing: One more swing thought for tomorrow. One more notion about putting. One more note to yourself about that hitch at the top of your swing.

And when you hit the rack, when you finally give your back some rest, you close your eyes and rethink your day. You visualize one shot. Then another. One hole, then another. As sleep comes, you resist. You aren't done yet. You're a golfer. There's always one more hole to revisit as you twist along your way.

(31) Giving It Up

THE THREE OF US STAND AT THE FIRST TEE. Planes rise above our heads from the nearby airport, noisily crabbing their way up into a viscous wind. I put my thumb to my ear. My brother is first up. He tees it up and says something. I'm sure it matters, but I can't hear. The wind. The planes. The traffic. The air is packed with sound, the scene bright and bone-dry. It's 7:15 AM. We are playing golf. This is Vegas with the wind blowing.

Despite the noise, the world looks remarkably empty from the tee box. The course—a new track called Bali Hai, situated just south of the Mandalay Bay Hotel—feels set down in this place, built just below the skin of the desert to keep us from seeing too much of the strip, or the airport, the highway or the parking lots, malls, drive-up tellers, table-dance joints, liquor stores, and billboards. The sky is painted the sort of blue that in other aspects of my life I reject for being—well—too blue. The blue of the T-shirt I never wear, of the rental car I won't drive, the blue in the lobby of my dentist's office. God-damned sky.

My brother hitches his pants. Now I can almost hear him. He's saying something about Siegfried and Roy or he's going on about Bloody Marys. I don't know which. He's knuckling down on a three-wood, trying to play smart through a southbound cross-wind. I do know just what he's thinking. Those first tee mantras: Control. Pace. Good posture. I couldn't care less. I'm three-and-a-half hours from quitting. Forever.

You will have to quit. Just face it. There will come a day when you just say the hell with it. Maybe you'll declare it's your last day. Maybe you'll know it in your mealy little heart. Maybe you'll plan to play this one last time, then take up jogging. Or maybe you'll just let the clubs lie around your trunk until you forget they're in there. Then it'll be Tuesday and you will realize, that's it. You're done. You were never any fucking good anyway. You never practice. And why the hell did you think the money, the time, all of it would make any difference? Just like that, you'll find that you have quit.

Today is my day. My head hurts, my neck is stiff, I'm out four hundred dollars from the tables, and my socks feel skanky. Now, my brother Frank, he cares. He's concentrating. Our partner—G.—he cares, too. He's also concentrating. He wants some of this. He's got his Liquid Metal driver out. He's eyeballing the distance like he's about to murder the horizon with a handgun. Me? I'm done. I can't make myself care.

Frank laces the ball and somehow it holds its flight, drifting a little only at the end. The starter whistles. I can see the sand rising up in little cones of wind from the traps. Behind us, a semi gears up.

Somebody is banging a pipe with a wrench in the distance. The starter nudges me with an elbow. "You see that green?" he says, pointing past the clubhouse, toward a tiny par-three.

I nod.

"That's where they did the *Playboy* shoot," he says. "Right fucking there. Twenty girls naked as the day is long." I take another look. An empty green. Beyond it, the course is crazy with palm trees.

Normally I'd make myself ask, force myself into some friendly invitation to one more chunk of local knowledge: Oh yeah? Right on the green? Were you there? He's just doing his job, after all. Making small talk. Gabbing. Just being a starter, helping guys knock the edge off their nerves. My lips are dry. And I left the chapstick on the dashboard of the car. Without thinking, I reach into my pocket, pull out a twenty, and give it to him. He looks at me like I've just handed him a sparrow.

"Thanks," I say, although I don't know why. The wind rips a wall between us and he can't hear.

"What do you need?" he says. That's just it. I don't need anything. And I don't know what I need. "I need a tee shot," I say, as that's the line most guys would use. He laughs and folds the bill.

Now G. tees it up, stares down the shot. Then I remember: He's the guy who taught me this. He insists that you can get on just about any course in America with a little patience and a twenty. Always tip the starter, he says. But this morning, we're on the course already; we're one shot into the round. That twenty made no sense, but I can explain. "I'm quitting," I say, leaning in. "This is my last round."

The starter raises an eyebrow and shrugs. "Too bad," he says. He's talking about me, about me leaving the game this one last time, and I am touched. One of the tribe is departing, turning his back on it all, and this guy is sorry to hear it. I want to explain. I'm not getting anywhere, I want to say. My game has flat-lined. I've taken to calling myself names after tee shots. Floppy, Flappy, Stubby. I've come to see myself as Stubby. I call myself Stubby in the off-hours. How can this be good? Nothing is happening. I'm standing on all these courses, in all these places, at the edges of all these greens, and I'm not rising up. Golf courses looked real to me. Once.

The day before, I'd played Shadow Creek with G. We'd wanted a look at Tom Fazio's masterpiece, the course built tree by tree in the middle of the desert, looking in the end like a lush Carolina mountain track. The course was littered with pheasants. On every tee box, we came upon a little warren of dwarf rabbits—tiny, friendly, narcoticized rabbits. Six to a hole, it seemed. You could reach down and touch them. All day long, G. knocked it straight, while I played like a potzer. I couldn't say why, except that I was thinking a lot about those rabbits. Where did they come from? How come they weren't overrunning the place? Did someone collect the extra rabbits?

It is too bad, I want to say to the starter. Thanks for seeing the sadness of it. I'm glad I gave him the twenty! But then I realize he can't hear me, that he's lamenting G.'s tee shot, which has settled into a fairway bunker. Another plane throttles upward, another roar, another glinting boatload of bodies. I reach in my pocket for a tee. So I start, leaning down, setting the peg, drawing back for a practice swing. "After this, Stubby is done," I say. "It's all over."

Frank smiles. "Stubby!" he says, as if greeting me for the first time. The wind eases. G. clears his throat. "Stubby better hit."

I laugh. Then I reach back, keep my hips in place, and turn on the ball. It jumps off the club, a little higher than I would like, and starts to fade. The wind holds it up a little, and in those few seconds there is absolute silence. The balls thumps down, center cut. I have drilled it.

I shrug. Frank slaps a hand on my shoulder. "Stubby always plays the fade like a master."

Before I start to tell him that I'm done, he leans on me a little. "I feel like shit," he says. "I'm not sure I can make it."

I laugh. "Sure you can," I say. "You ripped that ball."

He looks up, covers his eyes. "The sun, though. The wind. Jesus. Are we really playing again this afternoon?" he says, referring to our afternoon tee time at Paiute, the distant Pete Dye course where they say the wind never stops. He's wavering. I can see it, and suddenly I am not. The tee shot felt good. The grass is surprisingly wet. I'll have a seven-iron to a friendly pin, from a flat lie; I'm visualizing it even as we walk. Why would I walk away? There is nothing else I enjoy doing for more than an hour. Reading gives me a headache; movies are hit and miss. Watching television is like drinking water in the shower—pointless, wasteful, and kind of gross.

We're walking and I can now see that golf gives me some measure of the things I like in bigger chunks: Air. Conversation. Friends. A dim sense of labor. So I see the skeleton of the game once again. I'll hold Frank up awhile until he does, too.

I roll my shoulders, stretch a little, feeling what I can feel. We're off the box, out into the fairway. "After we quit here," I say, "we can grab a nap." Frank laughs. Now the blood is moving, the wind waning. Behind us, G. grumbles. I pull off my glove, retest my grip.

"Then we'll get out and go again."

"You sure you don't want to quit?"

"We can make it," I say. "We have time." This is true, too. We're after it. We're into it again. Now that the three of us are moving, I'm pretty sure there's no end in sight

$\left(32\right)$ The Perfect Storm

$IT'S$ THURSDAY AGAIN AND I'M ON THE FIFTH HOLE at my little club. My partners clump off ahead of me to better shots in shorter grass. Susan, who's been playing with us lately, is lying two, center cut, another fifty further on. Jere is a hundred yards better than that off his drive. Big Mike's tee shot lies a hundred yards lateral to me, though he's in the clear, so who can say? My tee shot was a little thin, and I'm staring at a five-wood on an uphill lie. Nothing remarkable. Just another Thursday. Except I'm four holes in, level par, aching to card a decent score, and there's been weather all day. At the moment, it's looking very ugly.

Things have fallen together the way they sometimes do in golf. At lunch back in town, near the office, I'd seen Wayne, my regular boy, looking miserable, hunched over a huge bowl of romaine lettuce. "Is Stubby going to hit some?" he asked, nodding at the window, at the air and the light and the fierce blue. He calls me Stubby only when we're playing golf, so I was surprised to hear it.

"Nah," I said. "You know. One meeting, then another." I bent down for a pretend look at the horizon. "Besides, there's weather coming."

Wayne nodded. "It's supposed to rain like hell tonight."

The truth is, I never watch the weather. Not on the news, not on its channel, not even in the distance. For me, weather drifts in the way teenagers pass me in the mall: often in surprising volume, generally from the same direction, and always indifferent to me. "Tomorrow?" I said.

Wayne took a forkful, looked deep into the business of his salad, and shook his head. "Rain," he said. "All day."

At moments like this, a day tilts. Wayne had pulled back the curtain on my golf self by calling me Stubby there in the restaurant, miles from the first tee. Hearing my golf name had the same effect as a flash of cleavage, bending my neck against the weight of the inevitable, unsealing the urge to shoulder a bag, to take my cut, to sneak away for whatever I could get. I work 1.3 miles from my home course. No meeting, no appointment, is sacred. This is my way. "Dammit," I said. "I'm playing."

Wayne smiled. "Stubby needs to play."

"Four o'clock?" I said.

"I wish." Wayne shook his head. "One meeting, then another."

Suddenly, I was testy against even the tedium of rearranging the day. I had to fight off the urge to go straight to the range for some important work with my eight-iron. The day had dawned some hours before, rife with the blood scent of achievement, looking like what it was: Work. Industry. Start early, get after it, finish late.

Now every tick in my appointment book looked heavy and swollen with the little tumors of obligation. So I cut into it all, trimming away, postponing, lying, leaving for tomorrow what I could do today, all the while patting myself on the back for keeping a change of clothes in the back of my car. Phone calls were made, a group formed, appointments rescheduled. I felt bad doing it. Lazy. Dishonest. Damned Wayne! Damned lunch!

And now, hours later, just as I've polished off my fourth solid par in a row, I'm staring down Stubby's specialty—a long, slippery fairway wood calling for a high fade to an elevated green—when what should come up but the weather.

The fifth hole at my little club sits on top of the whole world that is my little town. Look one way and you see the roof of the courthouse. In another direction—East? West? What does Stubby know?—there's a deserted ski slope. A river wanders through; a state highway bands it all together. From up here, the skies generally present themselves like a heavy, consistent sauce on the day.

Not today. Since the first hole, the weather has been different in each corner of the sky. When we teed off, patches of blue showed themselves over the town; huge, horrific thunderheads hung beyond all that. The clouds directly above us looked like big hunks of meat, while on the horizon they seemed as flat and gray as Lake Ontario. Hard to picture? Well, sure it is, because in fifteen minutes it would all be flipped around: the blue skies right over us, the meat clouds in the distance, the thunderheads inching closer. The world would swirl. All the while, I'm nutting the ball, hitting greens in regulation, just missing birdie putts. Stubby, playing like a champ!

I pull out my five-wood, rip a couple practice swings. I'm trying to stay focused. For some reason I keep hearing Johnny Miller, though I try to convince myself it's Johnny Mathis in an attempt to clear my head. I can't do it. He wants me to lock my left wrist. Or he's singing "Chances Are." Either way, it's not good. People are waiting. I swing.

Sure enough, I can't help myself and I block the ball, high and short. When I come up out of the swing—cursing myself and my own special inability to clear my own head of the empty voices of tipsters and crooners—lightning strikes.

I don't mean that it strikes in the distance or that we hear a distant rumble and groan in unison. I mean lightning hammers down on the earth somewhere near us, so close that the air is brightened by it. So close that I have a dim sense of electricity in the balls of my feet. So close that the only thing I can think to do is cover my ears and make eye contact with Big Mike, who is standing in the same position—hands over his ears, eyes wide, heels up off the ground. "Holy shit!" he says.

"Holy shit!" I echo.

And just like that, we hump it to the clubhouse, leaving our bags in a maintenance shed. By the time we get there, it's raining, even hailing a little, and we push into the clubhouse, shaking off the wetness. Immediately I try to force myself to give up, to accept that we won't be going back out there. Obligation beckons. But Jere wants to wait it out, and Susan, who has the bug real bad, would play through any kind of Old Testament weather at this point in her career. Hail doesn't scare either one of them.

The course hadn't looked the least bit full, but within minutes the clubhouse is crowded, the television flipped to the Golf Channel. One foursome sits down for a look. People take their spots at the tables, tallying scores, comparing handicaps, popping beers. Big Mike is talking wine. Susan tries on visors. People take practice swings, holding nothing but air. The whole world is there in that space, wearing ratty hats, gloves poking out of pockets, dressed in khaki, arms zip-zipping the microfibers as they talk.

The pro gives everyone a beer. On the television, one of the old guys makes a long putt. Jere can't take his eyes off it. "Look! Fluff is caddying," he says. "He's on the senior tour, caddying for Tom Watson! Fluff Cowan!"

Someone corrects him: "Tom Kite."

Everyone nods. Fluff is there, looping for Kite on some distant course where everyone is worried about the same things we are. The swing. The lie of the ball. Those distant rumblings. For a moment, this seems to matter.

By five o'clock, a shaft of sunlight shoots through the window of the clubhouse. This is when my day at work would normally end, when I would grab the things I usually grab, stuff them into the bag I generally use, and take them home to ignore for the night. All around the room, people crumple cans. The light widens, and when I walk to the window, I can actually see blue again. Better yet, I can see Wayne's car as he makes the turn into the club, fresh out of a meeting, driving in from under the rain.

It's as if the day has just begun. People pour out of the club into the wet sunshine, released into the weather. And once again, my world unfolds itself onto the golf course. The groups strip off rain gear, towel down their carts.

An hour ago, anyone would have called us fools. Leaving work early, walking off into the coming rain. This couple dozen of us—

who've hung in against the electricity, the rain, the heavy summer air—seem energized by the flip of the weather, by the chance for a few holes before dark, by our mutual faith, our willingness to persist. Now we'll close the day down on a golf course, slogging through the wet grass, watching the skies, humping out a few more holes before the next storm.

I tick back to my lie on number five. I'm sixty yards short, at the bottom of a valley, needing an up and down for par. In a minute, we'll grab Wayne and finish up as a fivesome. Wait until he sees my lie. I have a lot of work ahead of me.

THE AUTHOR

Tom Chiarella writes for *Esquire* magazine. His work has appeared in *Links*, *Washington Golf Monthly*, *Indianapolis Men's Monthly*, *The London Observer*, and *The New Yorker*. He has won awards from the Golf Writer's Association of America and the National Endowment for the Arts, and was a finalist for a National Magazine Award. He lives with his two sons in Greencastle, Indiana, where he teaches creative writing at DePauw University.

He is an eleven handicap. Barely.